LIFE AFTER ADDICTION

Leaving treatment can feel like being tossed into a strange new landscape without support, without knowledge of how to function well in this territory of sobriety and recovery. The landmarks may look familiar, but finding your way around feels utterly strange. People may call you by name, but your relationship to them has been changed by the experiences you've lived through. Somewhere in the middle of your life, often without any outward shift in scenery, you are starting over.

You will learn many skills for making your way socially through recovery. And you already know more than you think you do. You've been saying hello and good-bye to people for as long as you've lived. You've got many skills. This book will help organize them in your mind, and call upon them as you interact.

New
LIFE,
New
FRIENDS

Making and Keeping
Relationships in Recovery

Christina Baldwin
and
Cynthia Orange

BANTAM BOOKS
New York   Toronto   London   Sydney   Auckland

NEW LIFE, NEW FRIENDS

A Bantam Book / April 1993

Library of Congress Cataloging-in-Publication Data

Baldwin, Christina.
  New life, new friends : making and keeping relationships in
recovery / Christina Baldwin and Cynthia Orange.
      p.   cm.
  Includes bibliographical references.
  ISBN 0-553-35463-9 (pbk.)
  1. Recovering   alcoholics—Psychology.   2. Recovering
addicts—Psychology.   3. Interpersonal relations.
4. Friendship.
  I. Orange, Cynthia.   II. Title.
  HV5275.B38   1993
  616.86'1'0019—dc20   92-29813
                                                  CIP

Published simultaneously in the United States and Canada

Bantam Books are published by Bantam Books, a division of Bantam Doubleday Dell Publishing
Group, Inc. Its trademark, consisting of the words "Bantam Books" and the portrayal of a rooster,
is Registered in U.S. Patent and Trademark Office and in other countries. Marca Registrada.
Bantam Books, 666 Fifth Avenue, New York, New York 10103.

PRINTED IN THE UNITED STATES OF AMERICA

FFG   0 9 8 7 6 5 4 3 2 1

Whenever there is friendship,
there's a chance for human beings.

—ALEXANDER POPE

Contents

Preface

This book is a guide for building friendships for people stabilized in early stages of recovery or for people who find themselves cycling back through social issues and challenges. The information should be helpful for anyone embarking on new friendships or redefining and changing old friendships.

People have a heightened need for friends at critical junctures in their lives, during times of major turmoil and individual change. Recovery from addiction or dependence is one of the most dramatic changes anyone can undergo. It makes sense that our need for friends is at its greatest when we begin the recovery process and that the need to sustain friendship is ongoing.

This is an inclusive book. We are addressing people recovering from a variety of addictions and dependencies. We assume that our readers are in various stages of recovery: in treatment, just reentering the world, or having been working in the program for several years. While we often refer to the Twelve Steps, we recognize that many readers may be following other self-help approaches. Everyone has ongoing questions about making, keeping, and improving friendships. The book is written in simple, direct language, so that lifelong skills can be brought into focus and applied systematically.

We started this book as colleagues. We were writers who knew each other and who had spent time together in groups or at conferences. We finish this book as friends. We have tested many of the exercises, answered the questions, and lived with the concepts presented, both in befriending each other and in the other relationships in our lives.

In the course of writing, we asked recovering people what they felt were the most important elements to understanding friendship in recovery. We asked what they felt were the biggest hurdles to friendship, and why they thought friendships succeeded and failed in their lives. We interviewed friends, family members, and each other. Acknowledging the anonymity within Alcoholics Anonymous and other Twelve Step programs, we have disguised the circumstances and personal references of the authors of all bold-faced quotations and have used composites.

Acknowledgments

Thank you to our friends for letting us practice the imperfect art of friendship with you when it was so much on our minds. We talked about you a lot.

Thank you, cousin Rick, for the help and guidance you gave Cynthia and this project, especially in the early stages. Thank you, Judi, for the guidance you gave Christina. You tried to keep us on the track. Thank you, Michael. Thank you, Joy. You have many roles in our lives; the best one is "friend."

Christina Baldwin
Cynthia Orange

Minneapolis/St. Paul
Summer 1992

1

Coming into the World

Leaving treatment can feel like being tossed into a strange country with no knowledge of how to function in this new territory of sobriety and recovery. The landmarks may look familiar, but finding your way around feels utterly foreign. People call you by name, but your relationship to them has been changed by the experiences you've lived through—the fact of your past use, and the newness of your recovery. Somewhere in the middle of your life, often without any outward shift in scenery, you are starting over.

Just after I got out of treatment, I had this weird dream. I am being released from prison. I have just been given a new suit of clothes. This man walks me to the door, shakes my hand, and pushes me out. I stand on the other side of the threshold and look out onto a strange landscape. Nobody in sight. Behind me I hear the thunderous, metallic slamming of the prison doors. . . . Then I wake up. My first thought is "I sure hope there's somebody else out here besides me."

First Stage: Stranger in a Strange Land

There are three commonly defined stages of recovery, and friendship issues emerge in each stage. This book focuses on building friendships in stages one and two, when you've started a new life and need new friends.

In the first weeks and months of recovery, your primary task is to learn to find your way through an unfamiliar freedom. The prison doors in this man's dream may represent the imprisoning of his life to addiction. Now he's "out," but he doesn't know what to do next or who to find to help him.

There are many people in this new landscape of recovery. This book is aimed at helping those who are new to recovery, or those who are ready to deal with the social aspects of recovery, to find others in similar circumstances and become confident in the skills necessary for making friendships a celebratory aspect of a new life. If you are reading this book during the first stages of recovery, in the weeks following treatment, when entering a recovery group, or in early abstinence, you may need to deal first with your physical recuperation.

Before you can make new friends or reconcile and rebuild relationships with old friends, family, and coworkers, you need to cope with the physical debilitation and emotional upheaval of new recovery.

In *Restore Your Life: A Living Plan for Sober People,* Dr. Anne Geller refers to the first three months of sobriety as *convalescence.* During this time of physical withdrawal and intense emotional upheaval, your body and mind try to cope with the residual effects of drug use, food abuse, or alcohol consumption. Your first priority needs to be stabilization and physical recuperation. As Geller puts it:

You are recovering from a serious illness. You wouldn't expect to bounce back immediately from a heart attack or major surgery, and the effects of alcohol and/or drug dependency can take an equally grave toll on your body. Even though you are not bedridden, even though you may be able to hold down a job and care for your family, you must remember that you have a chronic, potentially life-threatening disease. The physical symptoms of withdrawal can be frustrating . . . allow your body the time it needs to heal.[1]

New recovery is like having a sunburn. You are tender and afraid someone will rub you where it hurts, so you back up and try to keep from getting bumped. But a little Solarcaine and someone to apply it in the places you can't reach yourself would surely feel comforting, so you step forward and hope someone will notice and offer to help.

You are not likely to have either the clarity or the energy to build new friendships during convalescence. This does not mean you have to struggle through this period alone. There are people in Twelve Step and other recovery programs whom you can call on for help and support, even before you become friends. If you have a core group of friends or family who have survived with you, ask them to help you get through these first months, and tell them what you need. For example:

• Admit what your physical symptoms are. Get reassurance from your doctor or group and tell your friends and family what is going on.

I can't sleep nights because I'm in withdrawal. It's like an adrenaline rush. My body hasn't stabilized without the drug. I'm sorry to be pacing the house.

———

My counselor says these crying jags will go away in a few weeks. Meanwhile, please don't think I'm crazy, I'm just having all the feelings I didn't have the past ten years. I'll settle down. That's what everyone in AA says.

• Tell those around you that they don't need to understand these symptoms and mood swings; the symptoms aren't part of a rational process. You do need, however, for them to accept these emotional and physical symptoms as "real" without assuming you will be this way forever.

Please be patient. I need to be immersed in the process. I know I'm obsessive about it, but it's the only thing really on my mind.

———

I know you miss me. I miss you too. Before, I was always going out using, and I'm still gone a lot because of all the meetings I attend, but this is my support for staying sober, and I gotta be there.

Question: What do you need to say to a family member or a friend that would help you right now?

_____

_____

_____

If it helps, write out sample statements, put them by the phone, and recite them to your friends and family. Convalescence is a period when you take care of your most basic needs. The people who have already stuck with you through addiction or dependence can probably hang on a little longer, especially if you communicate your awareness that you aren't really "back" yet and if you express a willingness to pick up your new life in stages.

Some friends and family members may have become dependent on your being the one with the problem. They need to go through a kind of convalescence of their own. Their reactions to your sobriety may surprise you and seem as erratic and unpredictable as your own behavior, symptoms, and mood swings.

During convalescence, you need people around you who have lived through similar experiences or who are genuinely sensitive to the recovery process. You need to be kind to yourself, too, to change the ways you have taken care of yourself, the things you have allowed yourself to do, to say to yourself, and to think about. Making a new life and establishing new friendships is a complex adventure. You can't do it all at once. If you are in the convalescence stage, relax. Convalesce.

This book is organized to help you think about friendship in a step-by-step fashion, building confidence and facing issues as they arise. Like the Twelve Steps, some points will be more meaningful to you at different times, while the overall framework remains important. Start where you are, build a solid context for change, and focus on the information and exercises that seem to be the most important aspects of friendship for you now.

Convalescence is the time to deal very directly with your own physical and mental recuperation. If people are threatening your daily commitment to sobriety or if they are threatened by the process, you may need to separate from them temporarily and get more of your support from recovery groups. If family members and close friends are willing to enter a support group of their own, it will help everyone adjust without any particular person having to bear the brunt of social demands.

Six Points for the First Six Months

In terms of this book, your social priorities could be expressed in the following list. You don't cover all six points in the first few months, but you can lay the foundation that will help you reconstruct your social life. When you don't know what to do, look at this list. Remember where you are and practice the point you are ready to practice.

1. Stay sober. Work the program.
2. Find a group of people who understand what you're going through and hang around them.
3. Relate to these people!
4. Be thoughtful about how you relate. Accept feedback. Try new behaviors. Move slowly, deliberately. Learn from your experiences without shaming yourself.
5. Develop a personal program using the exercises and suggestions in this book to test, reflect, write about, and celebrate your progress.
6. Practice. Practice. Practice. Dare to risk.

In convalescence, you begin to set the basic patterns of recovery. Recovery is not a process of making new rules, it's a process of learning new patterns for your life. Most of the work will be internal, but you may notice some external results. As you change, you help the people around you change. As you relate differently and more clearly, you offer others the opportunity to relate differently and more clearly to you. Sometimes this will be easy, sometimes difficult. It is not linear, not growth in a straight line. This list above is a reminder to walk the path *with others*.

As you read this book, do some of the exercises, and gain experience making sober friendships, you will gain confidence in your abilities to relate thoughtfully, to accept and learn from experience, and to celebrate the process.

6

Second Stage: Keeping Your Priorities Straight

The second phase of recovery might be called *feeling your way.* The most disastrous physical symptoms have usually subsided, and your emotions have settled down enough so you have a sense of social control. The enormity of the change you are making in your life may strike you.

> I remember a dream I had after I had been sober about four months. I am putting together a jigsaw puzzle, and every time I pick up a piece and think I know where to place it, the piece falls apart in my hand into even smaller pieces. And those pieces fall apart, until the pieces are so small I can hardly see them. It's really hard work, but I seem determined. Finally, I get a little corner of the puzzle reconstructed, and from the picture fragment I realize that the puzzle is my life. . . . When I wake up, I'm over-whelmed at how much I have to piece together. I thought recovery just meant to stop using.

During this stage, you may discover that the energy for friendship is beginning to return. You may also find yourself facing demands from people to pick up your social life. Others may tell you it's time to get on with your life and rejoin the community—at work, at leisure, at home. It's up to you to evaluate your own readiness and what you want "getting on with your life" to mean.

Everyone works their recovery to the best of their ability. Recovery isn't linear; recovery is circular, a wandering path of insight and determination that spirals around again and again past the same issues. There is progress in the spiral path: Every time you go by an issue, you see it from a different vantage point and have the opportunity to see what you have learned since the last time. As you pick up specific details and tasks of your life, you are likely to feel that you are back at the beginning. Not all of you is beginning anew, though you may feel like a beginner in one area or another.

My body was so ready to stop binging that going through sugar withdrawal actually felt good—even during the headaches and mood swings, the indigestion and shakiness. I could handle the physical symptoms, but I didn't know what to do with all the time I had on my hands. Most of my time had been structured around food. The worse my disease got, the more secretive my eating became. So, when I finally got help, I didn't have much of a social life. Food had become my best friend.

One of the primary tasks as you move through the second stage of recovery is the need to keep your priorities straight. There may be days when recovery seems to have little impact on who you are and how you conduct yourself, and other days when recovery is an overwhelming influence, seeming to invade every thought, every feeling, every decision, every action.

I kept trying to figure out my state of recovery by comparing myself to everyone else in a meeting. If someone sober over a year said something I agreed with, I congratulated myself for being so far advanced. If someone came in with three week's sobriety and said something that sounded like me, I was sure I was backsliding. I only wanted to relate to the stable ones, but I wasn't always stable myself. Finally, I just let myself be where I was: One day at a time.

Recovery is more than abstinence or making behavior changes. Recovery is the willingness to review everything: How you see yourself, your family, your friends, your work, your life. During this time, you are likely to feel intensely aware of these internal changes and your own sense of difference, and you may think everyone else notices as many changes in you as you are noticing.

> I felt branded, like Hester Prynne in The Scarlet Letter. I imagined myself walking down the street wearing a big capital A around my neck. Only the A stood for alcoholic. I took offense at any joke or reference to drinking. I fumed at advertising, the jolly beer drinking and romantic wine sipping on television. And whether this was true or not, I was sure that every friend I had thought of me as a freak, a failure. Someone not quite grown-up, someone who couldn't hold her liquor. I was defensive and sullen and angry at them, even if they didn't do anything to deserve it. I'd piss off a good friend on the phone, and then collapse on the couch and bawl because nobody loved me. I was a mess.

Everyone feels like a mess from time to time, and most of the time this feeling doesn't show the way we think it does. At these moments, it's important to practice befriending yourself. We are often more lenient, loving, and accepting of others than we are of ourselves. To be a good friend to others, we have to know how to be a good friend to ourselves. Chapter 10 focuses on befriending yourself, but you can begin now. Turn the exercises and dialogues suggested around to fit your internal befriending needs. Whenever dealing with someone else doesn't make you feel better, ask yourself how you need to apply a little friendship inside.

Question: Are you being kind to yourself? Take a moment and list the things you have done today to befriend yourself.

_____

_____

_____

There are several things you can do during the second stage of your recovery to help yourself feel more socially at ease and "normal."

• Tell your friends what you are ready to do and set conditions that you can tolerate with comfort.

Let's go to a football game, but I want to avoid the bar afterwards. If we go together, are you willing to eat with me someplace where they don't serve liquor?

• Give yourself permission to excuse yourself from any setting or event that triggers the compulsion to use, or which makes you uncomfortable.

I want to see this play, but sometimes I can't tell how emotional I'm going to get. Let's get seats at the end of the row, and then if I have to go out to the lobby for a while I won't have to crawl over anyone.

• Ask your friends for specific support.

I want to go to the league meeting, but don't let me volunteer for anything, and don't let anyone draft me.

• Use the guidelines in Chapter 2 to create a friendly community in Twelve Step or other programs.

Question: What is one specific form of support you can ask of a friend? Write it out, then go ask for it.

_____

_____

_____

Third Stage: A Rock to Stand On

According to Geller and others who have written about stages of recovery, *stabilization* occurs in the six- to twelve-month period of abstinence. This period is characterized by a kind of settling in. The understanding of recovery as a major life shift emerges from the sheer determination to stay sober. You are recovered enough to begin thinking about recovery as a new way of living your life and viewing yourself. This new life view requires that you restructure your thought process and way of handling emotions, as well as adopting healthier habits and abstinence.

In stabilization, friendship tends to become a major issue. Suddenly you blink aware and begin to notice what life in recovery can offer you. You can afford to relax some of the intense focus on yourself and see yourself as a member of a community, the recovering community. You begin to ease into social life.

• Take a look at how you spend your time. Perhaps you have gotten into a habit of isolation, except for attending meetings. Practice reaching out to other friends.

Hi. I was just thinking how I haven't seen anyone in six months, except other NA members. Do you still play racquetball?

• As you feel ready, shift your focus and offer to help others, to give back some of the support you've been getting.

You've been a trouper, letting me recover at my own pace. Now it's your turn for a little pampering. Let's go to dinner. I want to hear how Al-Anon is going.

• Begin to look at how you take care of yourself. Consider nutrition, exercise, and dealing with such habits as coffee or soda drinking and smoking.

• Use the exercises throughout this book to add the necessary social components for a rich recovering life.

Question: Now that you feel at least somewhat stabilized, what will your first step to friendship be?

_____

_____

_____

Life does not work like a textbook; plateaus are normal. You will find yourself resting at certain stages of recovery. You may have been abstaining for a long period of time and just be reaching stabilization, or you may be circling back to this point again.

I've been in recovery for years, but last week my best friend wrote me a letter and just said, "I'm done. Good-bye." I

called her right away and asked her to talk to me, and she couldn't. Couldn't put her feelings into words, just felt she had to totally withdraw. . . . Boy, that makes me feel like a beginner again. My mind is full of questions: What did I do wrong? Did I do something wrong? Why didn't I see this coming? What's going on with her that she can't even think about it? What's going on with me?

With each life experience, we have the opportunity to go back and reapply things we learned in earlier cycles. The Twelve Steps are used as a repeating program for a reason: Once is not enough. Understanding deepens every time we work a step, apply an idea, share our experience, and make a new friend.

This book does not tackle the breadth of the recovery process; it addresses two related concerns: *Now that you're in recovery, how do you find and approach the kinds of people you want to have as friends, and how do you maintain these friendships differently than you did in the past?*

Friendship is a verb, a process of finding out how you want to relate and how you want to be related to. Friendship is practice being with other people, learning from our interactions. **Friendship is a mutual and equal bond of respect, trust, and vulnerability that encourages healthy growth and acceptance.**

Right now, this definition may only sound like a bunch of words, but in the course of reading this book and practicing friendship skills on yourself and those close to you, these words will come to life.

So, Why Friends?

No matter how self-aware you are, the only way you can test your growth is through interaction with other people. Friends are the people we choose to help us grow; and friends are the people who have chosen us to help them grow. Friends see the world similarly, but differently. They help us have perspective. They fill in the pieces of human information missing from our own experience, and we help them fill in their missing pieces. Friends are living experiments in each other's lives.

This living experiment is connectedness. Human beings like to feel connected. We are, by nature, social beings. We live in groups. We feel safest around people we know. In recovery, many people you used to know and count on for your sense of connectedness may, for one reason or another, no longer be playing a significant role in your life. The other members of the softball team, for example, may have been more drinking buddies than teammates, and these friendships need to be abandoned or carefully redefined. You may have talked to your closest friends only after drinking too much or when you had unrealistic expectations of their ability to resolve your life problems for you. Now you are in the process of relearning how to connect without the distortion of drugs or alcohol.

When I was using, it was very clear who my friends were; they were the people I could get high with and the folks who provided me with dope. Now my friends are those who don't use and who help keep me from slipping back. But what we want from each other is a hell of a lot more complicated.

———————

People make changes at different times, and in their own ways. I have a good relationship with B., but there have been lots of changes over the years we've known each other. We go through long periods of time not being connected at all, but when one or the other of us is dealing with a major shift, we're right back in there—supporting, questioning, trying to be helpful and still staying out of the way.

In recovery, you will need to try out concepts, ideas, and ways of being yourself, alone, and in the company of others. Friendship in recovery *is* more complicated, because you are having to redefine many things at the same time. Early recovery is not exactly a calm and leisurely period of your life. At times you may feel that being a social creature only makes it harder. But overall, friends are good to have around, and practicing friendship is a happy process.

The Friendship Process

There is a loosely formed process to making friends in recovery. You—your circumstances, history, and friends—are unique. Making friends is not a procedure with prescribed rules. Making friends is a process that is both inner and outer. You reach out, interact, and then need to learn from your interactions so that you can take your insights into the next interaction. This process may be broken down into three types of activities: interacting, reflecting, and integrating.

Interacting consists of activities you do with others: noticing others, meeting and introducing them, inviting them to do things with you, spending time together, contracting and negotiating for further interaction, leave-taking and re-greeting.

Reflecting consists of activities you do separately or alone: thinking, questioning, writing, taking time out, and creating boundaries that fit the situation.

Integrating consists of activities you do alone and together: choosing self-esteem and mutual respect, learning without shame or blame, taking appropriate responsibility, claiming personal power, celebrating the process.

To practice a balanced friendship, you need to spend time in each of these ways, though one might seem most comfortable to you. Practicing friendship requires a different style of thinking and pattern of action from what you may be accustomed to. The greatest challenge of this book, and of recovery, may be the need to switch from following rules to thinking out situations for yourself, discovering what works and what doesn't. There are very few absolutes.

People around you are saying, "Don't use. One day at a time. Stay sober. Work the program," but *how* you follow this advice, how you practice recovery and rebuild your life and discover new friendships, will have a very individual character to it.

Life Is Good Practice; or, You Already Know More Than You Think You Do

Don't let this process scare you; you are already practicing these skills. Every interpersonal exchange fits somewhere in interacting, reflecting, and integrating. Every exchange is good practice.

The first three stages of early recovery are laid out by many authors and experts as occurring within the first year; however, early recovery doesn't just last months or a year. According to Anne Wilson Schaef and others, early recovery is a loosely defined period of time lasting three to five years. This is the time when you restructure your life, your living patterns, and your self-image. The social information in this book is inclusive and open to anyone who needs it—and you may need it, even when you think you won't.

Life is cyclical. Just when we think we've got a skill in hand, something happens to surprise us. Sometimes events turn for the better, giving us sudden increased confidence and the ability to drop an old anxiety. Sometimes events turn for the worse and an old anxiety suddenly returns to haunt us. We feel awkward all over again around a friend and need to review our boundaries and expectations. You will learn many skills for making your way socially through recovery. And you already know more than you think you do. You've been saying hello and good-bye to people for as long as you've lived.

Recovering support groups may not talk about the social practice they provide, but every time you go around the circle, work a step, or share an experience, greet another, offer support, and say good-bye until the next meeting, you are practicing your friendship-making skills. Since recovery groups are often the primary social outlet for the first stages of early recovery, they are a good place to start looking at how to make new friends for a new life.

2

Taking the First
Step to Friendship

Over fifteen million people participate in some form of self-help group in the United States. According to Nan Robertson, the author of *Getting Better: Inside Alcoholics Anonymous,* AA alone has almost two million members in sixty-three thousand groups in 114 countries around the world. And, Robertson says, AA's numbers double every ten years. People of every race, ethnic background and economic class, people of every religion and nationality, people who are atheists, people of every age group, men and women, are discovering what you are discovering: that the unconditional acceptance and support of others with similar problems is an essential aspect of recovery. These groups of peers are good, safe places to practice new friendship-making skills.

> When I walked through the door of my first Overeaters Anonymous meeting, I felt like I was eight years old on my first day of school. My stomach knotted up and my hands

got clammy. The people there knew each other and were chatting comfortably. I was the outsider, the one who didn't belong. When they told their stories, I thought, "That's not _my_ experience. _I_ never hid food in the bathroom so I could eat it in secret. _I_ never buried sweets at the bottom of my grocery cart so no one would see me buy them." Then someone said, "I used to think about food like my alcoholic brother said he thought about booze. I'd plan my day around it." A light went on in my brain and I began to pay attention.

You may have had a similar experience at your first Twelve Step or support group meeting. You may have felt out of place like the woman above, focusing on the differences between you and other group members, avoiding the similarities. When an accountant in a three-piece suit sits next to a leather-clad and tattooed biker at an AA meeting, the surface differences are glaringly obvious. But the shared desire to lead addiction-free lives mutes those differences. Your support group is a place you can be social, especially during the first stages of recovery— convalescence, feeling your way, and stabilization—even if you aren't ready to plunge into friendship building.

Recovery: Shared Journeys

When I got out of treatment, I felt so different. I thought everybody was watching me all the time. Even the simplest jobs got me uptight. Everything took longer and seemed harder because I was so afraid of screwing things up. I remember one day when I had to go to the grocery store. I waited in line wondering how all these people did it, how they were able to look so _normal_. Then this guy ahead of

me opened his wallet to pay for his groceries. Something
fell out and clinked to the floor. I stooped to pick it up and
was just blown away. It was a one-year medallion! When I
put it in his hand, I winked and said, "Me too."

There is a certain sense of comfort and affirmation when you
realize you are not alone. It feels good to see a medallion, a
butterfly pin, a bumper sticker that says HONK IF YOU KNOW BILL W.
or EASY DOES IT. You feel like you have something in common, even
with strangers. But what is it you share? How are you like a person
who attends AA in Sri Lanka? Knowing what recovering people
have in common will help you feel more socially at ease. It will
become easier to look behind the suit coats or leather jackets, the
diamond rings or the second-hand clothes, and see the understanding and companionship that surround you in this first circle
of potential friends.

Self-help meetings prove that the old adage "It takes one to
know one" is true. What you have in common with other recovering people includes:

- Determination to abstain
- Acceptance of addiction and dependency
- Dissatisfaction with the past and a desire to improve the
  quality of your present life
- Sense of needing to catch up
- Feelings of grief
- Need for a safe community in which to sort out confusion and
  get support.

This is a pretty dramatic list of commonalities. If you walked
into the company lunchroom, a church group, a social club, even
your family reunion, you might not have more than one or two

points in common with most of the folks there, *and* it would be harder and riskier to find out what you do have in common. In recovery, you can assume commonalities with others who attend the meetings and you can expect confidentiality. The social risk is lessened and safety heightened. No wonder these meetings often serve as the primary haven for recovering people.

The Determination to Abstain

Abstinence means different things to people recovering from different addictions. If you are recovering from addiction to alcohol or drugs, abstinence means *no use.* If you were addicted to food, abstinence means *no abuse.* As you recover from codependency or addictive thinking, abstinence means changing behaviors, beliefs, and patterns of rationalization.

> I stopped using. I stopped smoking. Sometimes I had to remind myself a hundred times a day: I don't drink. I don't smoke. I hated obsessing about abstinence as much as I hated my old habits, but everyone kept telling me this was just part of it. They were right, now I only have to remind myself ten times a day. [He laughs.]

In *Passages Through Recovery*, Terence Gorski says, "Every addict has two distinct sides: the addictive self and the sober self. The goal of recovery is to put the sober self back in charge."[1]

Maintaining abstinence—putting the sober self back in charge—is a tough job to do alone. For you, abstinence might mean eliminating alcohol or drugs from your life. For others, it means altering a compulsive behavior like addictive sex or gambling. For overeaters, abstinence might mean following a healthy meal plan free of foods that trigger binge eating. Whatever changes you need to make, you will find it easier to abstain if you have the support and understanding of those who also struggle to make similar changes.

Question: Have you found yourself obsessing? On what?

_____

_____

_____

Question: Name one person at your support group whom you could talk to. Do you have his or her phone number? How could you start a conversation with this person?

_____

_____

_____

For about four weeks in a row, A., a woman in my group, told me in great detail about the decor of a bar she used to go to. I remember thinking, "Here's somebody who gets as obsessive about topics as I do!" After the meeting, I told her I knew a coffee bar that had the same kind of feel to it and invited her to join me for a cup. It was easier than I thought. We ordered two espressos, and pretty soon we were talking about everything we could remember getting obsessive about, starting with hairdos and boys in junior high. We laughed at ourselves, and I began to settle down, to see that my obsessions and myself are separate. A. and I still get together to dump the buildup of obsessive thought. We think we're screamingly funny!

The Acceptance of Addiction and Dependency

When a person is addicted to something, s/he has an overpowering, repetitive need for some substance, object, feeling, or personal interaction—at any cost. The word *addict* comes from the Latin word for surrender. At the height of addictive behavior, people surrender their will to a drug or a behavior pattern. Recovery is a new kind of surrender: surrender to acceptance of help. Help from a Higher Power. Help from your "sober self." Help from a community of recovering friends.

> The first time I went to Al-Anon, I couldn't believe the variety of people there. I'd felt so alone for so long, and my part in my husband's drinking and in my son's cocaine habit was invisible to me. Al-Anon taught me that I could think about emotional behavior as clearly as I could think about their addictive behavior. It taught me to see that codependent behavior is as real as a bottle of liquor or a coke spoon.

Acceptance of addiction and dependence is a process of incorporating your history into your view of yourself, and defining yourself as larger than the addiction or dependence.

> I am an alcoholic, and much more. A mother, an ex-wife, a single woman, a working woman, a Lutheran, a bicyclist, an avid bridge player, a careful consumer. It's easy to get

acceptance for most of these things—and in Women for Sobriety, I know acceptance for my alcoholism and support for my recovery is always there too.

Question: How do you define yourself? Write out all the things that you are.

_____

_____

_____

Question: How do others define you in ways that you like? In ways that you don't like?

_____

_____

_____

The purpose of speaking in a group meeting is to practice community, to discover that you _do_ fit, and that you are accepted in this community as you are, no matter where you are in the process of recovery. Taking risks to share yourself builds confidence in your new self-definition and in your ability to sort through, to claim and reject, what others say about you.

In recovery, _you_ get to decide who you are and how you want to define yourself. You are developing a stronger and stronger sense of the "sober self," the self you can trust to guide your life and keep you in touch with others and with your Higher Power.

Dissatisfaction with the Past and a Desire to Improve the Quality of Your Present Life

In addiction, destructive behavior distorted the way you acted and reacted. Your life may have felt like a runaway train, fueled by compulsion, mowing down anything and anyone that got in its way. Now you're ready to get back on track. In recovery, you share a desire to learn from the past and to get beyond the past, to live fully in the here and now.

> One day, I remember dreading to get out of bed. I had to make breakfast for the family, pack their lunches, drive my kids to school, my husband to work, and then go grocery shopping for my mother—all before 9 A.M. because my friend was dropping off her two toddlers since her child-care worker was sick. I just started crying. I felt like everyone had a piece of me and there was nothing left for me. Not one minute. Later that same afternoon, I had to take my mother to the doctor, and as fate would have it, I picked up a magazine to read while I waited for her. A cartoon caught my eye in which one character asks another, "Do you know the definition of a codependent? . . . When they're dying, someone else's life passes before their eyes." I started to cry again. I want my life back.

For some people, putting your life in order may mean opening yourself to others and making new friends. For others, recovery may mean pulling back a little, giving yourself long-denied attention. For everyone, recovery means moving beyond unhealthy extremes to a new balance, to a place where we experience the mutual and unencumbered give-and-take of fulfilling relationships.

Questions: Do you find yourself stuck thinking "what if" or "if only," longing to reconstruct the past instead of coping with the present? How can your meetings help you concentrate more on "one day at a time"? Whom at your meetings can you talk to about this?

_____

_____

_____

Question: One way to overcome "if only" thinking is to concentrate on positive things. For each regret that creeps into your mind, list three current joys (don't list the regret). How did this exercise make you feel?

_____

_____

_____

A Sense of Needing to Catch Up

Most recovering people have been so weighted down by their addictive behavior that they experienced very little personal progress in the days before going to treatment or to a support group for help. Emotional maturity tends to get stunted at the height of addiction. If your addiction had an early onset and lasted for a number of years, you probably have some emotional and social catching up to do. You may feel like the world has been spinning without you and that the social rules have changed without your noticing.

My wife and I just coexisted with my drinking, and the women who hung out in the bars, well, liquor talked, but we didn't. Suddenly sober, I don't have any social skills at all. I mean, the women in AA are real, tough, challenging women. I like them—but, holy smokes, I sure don't know how to relate to them!

In the first stages of recovery, your reactions and emotions may seem outdated, adolescent, or inappropriate. As you may have already learned from others in your support group, this is a normal state. At recovery meetings, you can discover and practice how to develop appropriate, mature responses to different situations. These skills are easily transferable to relationships outside the recovery-group setting.

Questions: How is your inner self different from your outer self? How "old" do you feel inside?

_____

_____

_____

Questions: How can your meetings help you "grow up"? Whom at your meeting can you talk to, and how could you bring up this subject?

_____

_____

_____

Grief

Recovery is a process of letting go of many things: old friends, familiar behavior, addiction, your former self-image. As you let go, you grieve for alcohol or drugs and for the relationship you had with them; you grieve for lost hope—the hope that chemicals would make you feel better and fix your lost self-esteem. It may not make sense to grieve for something harmful, but we do grieve for it.

Grief is the emotion that flushes us out and makes room inside for real recovery. Grief allows deep changes to occur inside the self over time, so that new lives and new self-images emerge from the ashes. Allowing grief, even when we don't understand it, when it doesn't make sense, or we just feel sad with no way of explaining the feeling, is a way to befriend ourselves. The more readily you can allow grief to flush through you, the more readily you prepare inside for new experiences to fill you up again.

Three months out of treatment I remember a period of time when I'd come home from work, curl up on the sofa, and cry for about twenty minutes. Then I'd turn on music and find myself dancing. I thought I was crazy, but it felt exactly right. Crying, dancing, then off to AA.

Grief and celebration are two sides of the same coin: We grieve changing and we celebrate changing. Grief is where we start from, and new friends—those in recovery groups down the street and around the world, friends we haven't even met yet—are those with whom we can share our grief and our dancing.

Questions: How have you felt sad, angry, or confused about the losses you've experienced or the changes you're making? Whom at your meeting could you talk to about grief?

_____

_____

_____

A Need for a Safe Community in Which to Be Confused

A recovery or support group meeting is a sanctuary, a safe place where you and other recovering people can express confusion, ask questions, and explore options. If you are new to recovery, you may feel unsure how to cope in a social setting without the buffer of whatever substance or behavior consumed you and took the place of authentic interaction. Especially in the first six months, a caldron of long-denied and overlooked emotions may spill over, alternating with stretches of time when you don't feel anything at all.

> In group, someone challenged me to "name the fear." I could not. Instead, I talked about a friend who was falling apart, crumbling inside herself. "Is that your fear? That <u>you</u> will fragment?" a woman asked me. My tears surprised me. They were overlooked tears, old tears, tears I thought I had cleverly hidden. The members of my eating-disorders group draw them out, gently. Sharing my pain with them is a better way to bring up the truth than the bulimia which brought me to them. Sometimes I feel like the emptiness within me—the familiar black hole I used to fill with

29

food—will become me and I will disappear. This is my fear. That I will disappear and no one will notice.

When you decided to get better, you entered treatment or went to your first step meeting as an "I." Immediately upon walking through that door for help, however, you became part of "we." The language of recovery is an inclusive language. Step One of the Twelve Steps says, "*We* admitted we were powerless, that *our* lives had become unmanageable." Recovering people need other recovering and supportive people in their lives—even though it's scary to let others see the new self that is emerging.

Question: What are you confused about, fearful of, grieving for, right now?

_____

_____

_____

Using additional paper, set a timer and write for five minutes. Get your feelings on the outside so you can feel better on the inside.

At meetings, you interact with peers. In this safe community, you don't have to wait to get your needs met, to ask for a response or to respond to others. Take consistent little risks: Look someone in the eye while they talk, nod your head in agreement, pay attention to someone else. When you take risks like this, you practice being a social person. You don't have to have the answers to someone else's dilemma; in fact, it's better if you don't. You just need to be present, to show up with your mind as well as your body.

Questions: What could you offer a group member who is working through some of the same issues as you? How can you approach this person?

_____

_____

_____

Your Support Group Is a Testing Ground for Sober Friendships

In your support group, you can learn many things about human interaction which will help you immensely as you make new friends and clarify old relationships. By observing how recovery group members set limits, establish healthy boundaries, express emotions, and handle the ups and downs of everyday life, you can think about how you want to live. Then, during the hour or so you are together, you can practice these new living patterns in a safe and nonjudgmental environment. You can express needs and fears and test whether or not these needs and fears seem reasonable to others. At first you might feel like a sponge, soaking up everything you hear at your meeting, but you will soon learn to "take what you want and leave the rest."

This simple phrase is a very sophisticated concept. It requires clear thinking which you may not have yet, and the ability to reflect on what people say to you and how they behave. Throughout this book you will be invited to experiment with others, to practice *interaction*. You will also be encouraged to practice *inner action*, to experiment within yourself, to be reflective, to practice thinking about *who* you are and *how* you are with others.

31

When you practice effective *interaction*, you learn to give and accept feedback. The purpose of feedback is to validate and expand your view of what's going on in a nonjudgmental way. Nonjudgmental feedback uses "I" statements rather than "you" statements. For example, "I don't understand the point you're trying to make" is nonjudgmental; "You're not being clear" is judgmental.

Feedback is often a surprise, a shock to the ego, like reaching the end of a rope you didn't know you were tied to. When this happens, you may have a tendency to respond with shame or anger—to protect yourself against the surprise. You may be afraid to accept feedback, to let yourself be influenced. This is why you need the reflective part of the friendship process. Reflection allows you to go off by yourself and think about what has just happened.

Learning to perceive and receive feedback, to take what fits and leave the rest, even when it is well intentioned, is a long process in recovery. You can't just magically "get it right"; you need to learn to sort and reflect upon what's been said and then integrate what feels appropriate. Here are some exercises for receiving and using feedback from others:

• When you speak, explain to others honestly how you are feeling and ask if they've had similar or different reactions.

> My anger was off the chart at work the other day. I was busting my butt to meet a deadline, and this guy I work with just screwed off all day. He made about five personal phone calls and I didn't even have time to take a break. I stayed mad all day and cried like a baby when I got home. Has that ever happened to you?

• When others respond, listen attentively (and nondefensively) to their reactions and experiences.

32

> That happens to me a lot at my job. I used to get pissed off
> and slip into a martyr role. I'd be real nice and work all the
> harder, hoping my colleague would get the message. Try-
> ing to control how she acted just made me tired and
> angrier. Now I figure that what she does is none of my
> business.

• Think about what's been said and, if it seems helpful, apply
what fits for you.

> I guess I was wasting a lot of energy on how I thought he
> should be doing his job. Maybe he didn't even know I
> needed help. I guess I could ask him to help me next time
> and see what happens.

Most self-help meetings are conducted in a nonthreatening
atmosphere. Generally, members are listened to respectfully
without interruption, and feedback is given when it is requested
but limited to the issue at hand. Giving advice is discouraged,
since all members are fellow *seekers*, not teachers or sages. In a
recovery group, you journey together. Offering and accepting
feedback is an exchange that requires thoughtfulness by all the
people talking.

When you start watching how they act and interact, you'll
probably notice that even long-time members of your group say
they are often mystified by what "normal behavior" is. It is a
common assumption among recovering people that "normal"
means everybody else. Since addiction and dependency are often
multigenerational patterns among families and friends, we lack
constructive models for learning how to interact. Learning to
interact is the basis for friendship and the underlying skill you will
gain from experimenting with the exercises offered in this book.

Everyone in your recovery group is engaged in the experiment of rebuilding their lives. When you ask for feedback, think about what fits your values and matches the complexity of your situation. As you think about things and listen to yourself talk, as well as to what others are saying, you'll realize that you possess the most complete understanding of your own situation and are best qualified to judge what feedback is appropriate and constructive. Feedback broadens our horizons about an issue, but it doesn't replace our own knowledge. Remember that when you offer advice, you are the newcomer to the thought process, and the other person is the expert. Share what you know and give the other person plenty of room to make up his or her own mind. Your support group is a testing ground; that means it is fluid, changing, growing in awareness, just like you are.

> I used to get so defensive about what anyone would say to me that I would never ask for feedback at meetings. Finally, I devised this mental system I called "The Clearing Room." Whatever someone said to me, I put it into the Clearing Room, and when I was alone, I'd picture myself going in there and deciding, word by word, what fit, what I would accept. I don't need to do that anymore, but it gave me enough inner control to listen to what others had to say.

Question: What recent experience with feedback has turned out to be positive for you? Describe the situation and what you learned.

_____

_____

_____

Taking Care of Yourself

The real genius of the Twelve Step model is that it was the first genuine peer group. The founder of Alcoholics Anonymous took the risk to declare that other alcoholics, operating in groups where leadership changed on a meeting-to-meeting basis and every person's experience made him or her a resource to everyone else, provided the best support for recovery. This assumption has proven so valid that it has shaped the development of the entire self-help movement.

As a newly recovering person, you are entering into a contract among peers when you go to a meeting. You are agreeing to accept support and feedback and to give support and feedback. The multiple meetings you attend in the first weeks out of treatment or in the first weeks of recovery may not feel like the right places to make your group home. As you enter the stabilization phase, you need to find a solid, ongoing meeting that is compatible with you and meets your needs. You may go through a transition period of "shopping" for the right meeting.

Question: Now that you've had some experience with different groups and settings, what characteristics of a meeting would be right for you?

_____

_____

_____

The following subjective criteria may help you think about what you are looking for in a meeting:

- **You Need to Feel Safe.** Seek a comfortable and dependable meeting with at least several regular attenders.

- **You Need to Be Able to Ask for Feedback Without Fear of Being Abused or Manipulated.** Half of this interaction is your responsibility.
- **You Need to Be Discerning.** Do not put yourself in the position of indiscriminately accepting everything the group says. Trust yourself. You may be new to recovery, but it is *your* recovery.
- **You Have the Right to Choose.** You may want to give a meeting several trial visits until you discover its core membership and how you fit into the makeup of this particular meeting.

You will not do this perfectly. You will go through periods when you tend to be overly defensive or overly trusting. Right now, the most important thing is to find a meeting or several meetings that assist you in the early stages of recovery where you can gain experience in interacting, reflecting, and integrating.

I found an Al-Anon meeting I liked and went for six weeks, and then this guy came back from vacation. I could tell he was a regular by how the others greeted him, but the group seemed unusually quiet. After he had made a long comment, I tried to add a perspective from my own family history. The man became extremely challenging. His verbal violence reminded me of my own father, and must have reminded other folks too. Suddenly, I was the "mom," he was the "dad," and everyone else in the group was scuttling for cover the way they had as kids. I went back to the next week's meeting and stayed as quiet as the others while I watched him carefully. I decided I couldn't get what I wanted in a meeting where he was the dominating presence, and I didn't want to engage in a power struggle for leadership. I just changed meetings. It felt really healthy for me to decide that this wasn't my battle.

Question: How have you changed a response to interaction or feedback in a way that feels good to you? Describe the situation and what change you made.

_____

_____

_____

While looking for a meeting you like, you need to keep your priorities straight. The peer group aspect of recovery programs will challenge you again and again to practice seeing clearly your own behavior and the behavior of those around you. It may be tempting to seek a group of people very similar to yourself, but diversity can be a very good learning tool. You can learn a lot by watching people who seem unlike you and by watching how different people interact.

> There is a woman at the meeting I go to who only sees the bright side of any situation. She even calls herself Polly-anna. Then there's this guy who is just the opposite—he expects that "shit happens." They're great together because they have such totally different approaches. Inevitably, after I listen to them both, I discover an answer somewhere in between.

Too Close/Too Far: What Is a Boundary?

It is impossible to talk about friendship without talking about boundaries, because much of the work and play of friendship-making is about boundary-setting. The dictionary defines a boundary as "something that indicates or fixes a limit or extent."

Have your boundaries tended to be stone walls? Rigid rules? Lines you let others cross without even noticing?

Appropriate boundaries are the way you differentiate yourself from others; they protect and preserve your individuality and help keep your self-esteem intact. Since recovering people tend to operate at extremes, you may be accustomed to operating with few boundaries, opening yourself to people you hardly know, or you may be used to operating with rigid boundaries, shutting out even those who care for you the most.

In addition, we tend to behave in a polarized fashion. We fear smothering or abandonment. We feel overwhelmed with emotion or devoid of feeling. We swing through moods of elation and despair. In recovery, these polarized behaviors and reactions are challenged and brought into balance. You and everyone else in your meeting are in the process of moving from an extreme that represents the addictive self to a balance point that represents the sober self.

Questions: When you were using, what were you afraid would happen in your relationships with others? What behaviors did you use to avoid this fear?

_____

_____

_____

Question: What is the balance point you think you are aiming for in recovery?

_____

_____

_____

The polarities of addiction have led to many theories about recovering people and their boundary issues. In *Co-Dependence: Misunderstood, Mistreated,* Anne Wilson Schaef says, "Co-dependents literally do not know where they end and others begin."[2] This is an extremely loose sense of boundary and selfhood.

In his book *The Addictive Personality,* Craig Nakken says, "[the addictive personality] . . . forces them to withdraw, to isolate themselves from others."[3] This is an extremely isolated and often fearful sense of boundary and selfhood.

In *Families and Family Systems Therapy,* Salvador Minuchin calls a family with no boundaries or blurred boundaries an "enmeshed" family system. If a family has rigid boundaries, Minuchin says the family is "disengaged."[4] Enmeshed family systems tend to produce people who think fuzzy boundaries are normal, and they behave accordingly. Disengaged family systems tend to produce people who think isolation is normal, and they behave accordingly. Neither of these positions is a happy one, and in recovering friendships, you will have many opportunities to practice discovering a middle ground.

Minuchin says we travel through life on a continuum that looks like this:

DISENGAGED	CLEAR BOUNDARIES	ENMESHED
(Inappropriately rigid boundaries)	(Raising and lowering expectations to fit the situation and the level of relationship of the people involved)	(Inappropriately diffuse boundaries)

The goal in recovering friendships is to learn to operate as much as possible with clear boundaries. For most recovering people, the middle ground is a new experience, and like all new experiences, sometimes it is exciting and sometimes it is fearful.[5]

Being disengaged or enmeshed is a habit of thought and behavior. These habits seem normal until they are challenged, and new, workable options are offered. As you observe the people around you, at home, at work, and in meetings, and as you become aware of your own reactions to what is going on, you will discover which habits have been most familiar to you and from which position you are moving to middle ground.

Questions: From where on the continuum do you think you usually operate? What are the familiar behaviors and thought patterns that accompany this position?

_____

_____

_____

Enmeshed or Disengaged?

Look quickly at the following list. Put a check mark beside the statement that most often applies to you:

☐ I plan my time carefully and don't like interruptions unless they've been agreed to earlier.

☐ I don't care when people call or drop by; if they need help or want to talk, I'm here.

☐ The hardest thing about recovery is this group stuff. I don't want to get involved with everybody's life story.

☐ I never knew there were so many people like me. I've got all these new friends. We talk all the time, helping each other work the program.

☐ If I have a problem, I like to work it out myself.

☐ I like to find out what other people think and get their advice.

☐ My work is the most meaningful part of my life—what gives me esteem.

☐ My relationships are the most meaningful part of my life—what gives me esteem.

If most of the statements you checked are in the left-hand column, you learned to be disengaged. If most of the statements you checked are in the right-hand column, you learned to be enmeshed. If you had trouble putting yourself in one column or another, then you are ready to explore middle ground. Perhaps the following statements are beginning to describe you now:

☐ I like to be close *and* I like to be alone.
☐ I want to negotiate with others and have my needs respected.
☐ I respect my own time and the time of others. If I want to see someone, I always ask first if this is a convenient time.
☐ I enjoy the support I get at my meeting and practice listening to people without having to "fix" their problems or being afraid to hear what they have to say.
☐ When I have a problem, I think for myself and get advice when I need it.
☐ My relationships *and* my work both give me meaning and esteem.

How to Know if You're Ready to Take the Next Step

When you first start a recovery program, your life pretty much revolves around it. In AA, it is often suggested that newcomers attend ninety meetings in ninety days to reinforce their initial sobriety. Other recovery programs also encourage newcomers to attend frequent meetings and to read daily meditation books and other appropriate literature. Especially in your first months of recovery, your support group can be a lifeline to abstinence—even when you're not at a meeting.

> I heard a man explain abstinence to some newcomers. "Abstinence is what you'd do if you had all of us around watching you," he said. That made so much sense to me. Now, when I feel the urge to do something that would sabotage my program—binge with food, withdraw and isolate myself, contact an unhealthy person from my past, whatever—I imagine my group members watching over my shoulders.

Although during stabilization some people stay immersed in recovery programs to the exclusion of all else, most recovering people settle into a rhythm of attending one or two meetings a week. When you feel it is safe to let your attention to yourself lift a little, you are probably ready to start connecting with others in a more relaxed social atmosphere.

> I had been going to AA for about three months when I felt curious about other group members, wondering about their lives outside of group. Some nights I had to force myself to keep from interrupting when someone was sharing an experience. I wanted to jump in and say "Me too!" and ask them all sorts of other questions, not necessarily related to that night's topic or even to dependency.

Being curious about other people's experiences and wanting to share your own experiences are signs that you are ready to explore making friends. This does not mean you aren't still afraid.

It may be scary to approach someone, ask them out for coffee, open yourself and face possible rejection, but being ready to explore friendship means being ready to take risks. Risk is the opportunity to use your fear to step forward, to move toward what you desire.

Recovery support groups may not talk about the practice in social skills they provide, but every time you go around the circle, work a Step or share an experience, greet each other, offer support and say good-bye until the next meeting, you are practicing friendship-making skills.

As you consider the following questions, you have the opportunity to notice all the little social risks you're already taking and the movement you are making toward middle ground. These ordinary interactions form the basis for friendship-making that will be explored in following chapters.

• What does it feel like *now* to enter the room at your meetings?

_____

_____

_____

• Do you like the way you greet people? Does it feel natural? Are you comfortable?

_____

_____

_____

• Do you like how people greet you in return? What do you like or not like about how certain people greet you?

_____

_____

_____

• How honest do you feel about what you say in a meeting?

_____

_____

_____

• Are you more or less honest in a meeting than in other places in your life?

_____

_____

_____

• Can you name three people at your meeting you can really talk to about the early stages of recovery? Who are they?

_____

_____

_____

• How do they listen differently from others, or what do they offer that others don't?

_____

_____

_____

- Have you ever spent time with them outside your meeting?

_____

_____

_____

Though there is sometimes debate about whether or not recovery group members should develop friendships independent of the time they spend in meetings, it is common for members to adjourn the formal meeting and carry on the socializing at a nearby restaurant. Do not be afraid to join these informal sessions. They are good further practice in developing your social skills.

3

Old Friends

Recovery is not an exact science. Everyone recovers at his or her own speed in his or her own way. Assessing and redesigning old friendships is something we do throughout our lives, not just during the early stages of the recovery process.

Recovery means change. You are altering how you think, act, and feel about just about everything. Your relationships are changing too. You are learning to seek new friends who support your commitment to recovery and personal growth. And you are in the process of assessing old friendships, figuring out which people from your past will enhance your recovery and which people may threaten it.

Rebuilding Your Life

Suppose you've been in recovery about six months. There are people you used to spend a lot of time with whom you don't see very much—or at all. Some of these people were in your life as part of your addiction. They supplied you with drugs or alcohol or excused your eating habits or let you control their lives or tried to control yours. When you think of them, you have no desire to reconnect or you have a healthy fear about reconnecting.

However, there may be people you haven't seen whose role in your life is not so clear cut. They served you alcohol or cake at their parties, but your friendship wasn't based on that. You think there may be something to salvage. Perhaps they have written or called you, wanting to know how you are. You haven't been sure how to sort out the good aspects of these friendships and see if you can bring them into your recovery.

Old friends often represent a range of behaviors, activities, and interests. It's harder to separate out the support for your changes and recovery in relationships that include years of addiction, and yet these people may offer you a sense of continuity and a chance for acceptance both as you were and as you are now. Reassessing old friendships is worthwhile work in the early stages of recovery. Do this at your own pace, but do it.

- You don't have to call everybody you ever knew.
- You don't have to deal with all your old friendships right now or at once.
- You can deal with the easiest people first.
- You can keep practicing boundaries and renegotiate old friendships when you feel ready.
- You can renegotiate with the same friend more than once.
- You can take your own time. Even if old friends press you for explanations or decisions, it's perfectly fine to say, "I'm not ready" or "I don't know."

Sometimes, when friends don't call or you don't call them, it means the energy of that friendship is naturally fading away. Many—in fact, most—friendships have some sort of life span. Something brought you together: a mutual interest, children of similar ages or in similar activities, an emotional need—conscious or unconscious—that you (and they) were ready to sort out. When these agenda are fulfilled, the energy wanes and the friendship loses its importance. This does not mean anything is wrong, only that life is moving each of you along. If we didn't allow this to happen, our social lives would become unbearably complex and overcrowded. There wouldn't be room in our lives for new people or new experiences.

Question: Can you think of a friendship where the fading away felt natural and nontraumatic? Describe the situation.

_____

_____

_____

Question: What did you learn from this natural fading that you can now apply to situations with other friends?

_____

_____

_____

Dealing with old friends and clarifying or leaving old friendships is a part of the process of rebuilding your life. Choosing whether or not to continue working on a past relationship is an important part of recovery. The better your choices are, the more solid your recovery will be.

You may want to impose a kind of order on how you do this so you can see your own progress. You may want to walk through the following four steps at your own pace:

1. Respond to those people who are contacting you and establish *your* timetable or boundaries—not theirs.

2. Work the exercises in this chapter to identify and prepare to reapproach people whom you want as an integral part of your life and who will support your recovery.

3. Define, with support, those people you are less sure of and whom you may need to see or contact in order to clarify your relationship, to discover whether they can support your recovery or whether you need to find ways to let your friendship fade or end it.

4. Make a list of people you've lost track of but with whom you want to reconnect, to make amends, or to say good-bye.

Redefining Friendships

You probably started this discernment process about friendships when you decided to get help. When you entered treatment or counseling or started attending a self-help or Twelve Step group, you intuitively sought out people who could identify with your problems, support your abstinence, and provide models of recovery. As you move through stabilization, as you move from activities and relationships beyond your primary recovery meetings, you will find it necessary to rethink, and in some instances redefine, these past friendships.

In Chapter 1, friendship was defined as **a mutual bond of respect, trust, and vulnerability that encourages healthy growth and acceptance.** This new definition provides a clear standard for assessing preexisting friendships.

Some people may have a number of old friendships that seem fairly easy to redefine; some people may have none. Several factors may account for this difference. One factor is the length of time a person was deeply involved in addiction and the deterioration of the rest of his or her life. People who addressed their addictions, or whose family and friends provided early intervention, are likely to have more intact friendships than people who suffered the advanced stages of use.

> Many members in my family are chemically dependent, so when my drinking started to get out of control, an alarm went off and they got me into treatment right away. Some of my friends were totally bewildered, but coming from my family—even I knew the signs.

If your addiction was quite advanced, you may have abandoned nonusing relationships in favor of ones with people who participated in addictive habits.

> When I went into treatment for cocaine addiction, I realized I had alienated myself from everyone I cared about. I hadn't seen my racquetball buddies for over a year. I didn't know if the softball team I had played on every summer since law school even got together anymore. Sarah and Mike and I used to have brunch every Sunday and talk about everything: politics, love. . . .
> Before treatment and NA, the only people I saw were other cokehead attorneys who partied with me, sometimes for days at a time. By the time I got into treatment, I had lost my job and all my real friends.

Another factor is whether your preexisting friendships were made by your "addictive self" or your "sober self." Even during your advanced addiction, remnants of the sober self may have been available for you to use to build friendships. Relationships that accommodated your addiction, while certainly influenced by addiction, may have enough healthy aspects to them to make redefinition highly possible.

I guess I knew Mary drank too much, but I almost never saw her do it. I never binged in front of her either. I was this mysteriously fat person who always ordered salad, and she was the temperate drinker who had only one wine spritzer and mysteriously went to bed drunk. When we both got into treatment, we were able to define all the good stuff in our friendship and change the old patterns of denial.

First Things First

To sort out whom you want to see, whom you want to keep as a friend, what you want to say to a friend and how to say it, think about your preexisting friendships. List the friends by name. Have they contacted you, or have you contacted them? Do you want to see them? Do you need to see them? Why?

Friend	Recent contact?	Want to see?	Need to see?	Why?

People You Do Not Want to See

As you look at your list of friends and the checkmarks and comments, start with the people with whom you have had recent contact. If you have not checked that you want to see or need to see these friends, you may want to let them know that you need more time to sort things out before you get together with them. Develop a telephone script if you need to, or compose a postcard. If it helps, refer to the boundary section in chapter 2.

Questions: What kind of boundaries (enmeshed? disengaged?) did you keep with them when you were using? How did these boundaries play out between you?

_____

_____

_____

If you tended to disengage, you might be tempted to write a terse note: "Please don't call me," offering no explanation. If you tended to become enmeshed, you might be tempted to write a ten-page letter overexplaining yourself, then, if anticipating hurt or anger, trying to patch things up.

Question: How do you think your habits about boundaries might affect the way you try to resolve old friendships?

_____

_____

_____

Question: What could you do differently?

_____

_____

_____

Question: Why do you or don't you want to see this person?

_____

_____

_____

You cannot predict or control how a friend will respond to what you have to say. Your task is to communicate as clearly as you can, and to take responsibility for *only your* actions. If it feels comfortable, you could say or write something like

> Thank you for calling to see how I am; I really appreciate your concern. I am still sorting out how I feel and what changes I need to make in my life. When things settle down, I'll be in touch; take care in the meantime. I'm thinking of you too, and it's nice to know I'm not forgotten.

If you're having trouble thinking of ways to ask for more time or distance from old friends who may be calling you, ask your recovery group members or other friends for help.

ou Do Want to See

.endships you *want* to maintain are most likely those that have a good basis for redefinition. If a preexisting friendship grew out of mutual healthy interests, you may both want to continue the friendship and find that your recovery is easily absorbed into these already healthy patterns.

> Pat and I have been close friends for over twenty years. We worked together, saw each other through stormy marriages. I hid her under my bed when her ex-husband came looking for her in a drunken rage. We cried for each other when our children were born, were there for each other during painful divorces and happy remarriages. We're like this crazy kaleidoscope. We keep rearranging, repositioning, and redesigning ourselves, yet always remain connected to the middle somehow, no matter how changeable the pattern.
>
> Pat probably knows me better than anyone, yet I didn't tell her about my bulimia until after I got help for it. When I finally did confide in her, she accepted the news unwaveringly, then asked for clarification of her role in my recovery. "So, do you need me to listen at the bathroom door?" she asked, grinning a little nervously. We both burst out laughing at that image and got on with the business of being even better friends.

In these types of old friendships, channels of communication and connection that can absorb new information have already been established. The primary change is to make sure your old friends acknowledge the importance of your recovery. You may need to educate them about the issues most important to you, about the Twelve Steps or aspects of your particular recovery program and about the impact you expect recovery to have on how you spend your time with them.

Old Friends

When you connect with old friends, it is important to remember that what you are dealing with is *mutual confusion*. You are emerging as a new person, and your change creates change in them. They are likely to be nervous too, to greet you with their own hopes and fears. They may not know what to say to you, whether or not to ask you about recovery, whether you are interested in what has been happening recently in their lives. A period of awkwardness is normal. The first reconnection with an old friend is usually a threesome: your friend, yourself, and the ghost of your former self. You can exorcise the ghost by planting yourself firmly in the *present*, staying in the here-and-now, and consistently relating what you're doing *today* regarding recovery.

The more comfortable you are at being yourself now, and the more able you are to talk distinctly about the differences between the past and the present, the more comfortable your friend is likely to be as well.

Much of this awkwardness occurs because there is no longer a mutually understood framework for social behavior. You may need to agree upon new social rules. A recovering alcoholic may ask her friend not to drink in front of her in the first months of recovery. A recovering compulsive overeater may ask his friend not to order dessert when they go out to dinner. They may change these guidelines later, but for now it gives each friend a way of signaling support, and a specific behavior change upon which to build the new relationship.

Question: What three things do you need to say first in anticipation of seeing _____ ?

1. _____

2. _____

3. _____

Question: What one behavior change in the friendship would make you feel most comfortable?

_____

_____

_____

Question: Is there a behavior change you are willing to make to help set your friend at ease?

_____

_____

_____

If your friend is not in recovery, you might need to explain what is going on, or help him or her understand the new vocabulary you speak—the mottoes and slogans that are helping you— one day at a time. Reconnecting with preexisting friends is a practice in empathy: You want them to be able to accept and understand who you are now, and you need to be ready to respond to what they want from you too.

People with whom you have less intimate friendships may also appear on your "want to see" list. If you have a friend who is your movie-going partner, your bowling buddy, a car-pool friend, a coworker, neither of you may be exactly sure how your new definition of yourself as a recovering person fits into the relationship. You have a right to decide who among your old friends needs to be aware of your recovery so that you can get the support you need. You also have a right to decide who does not need to be involved.

Probably by the time you read this, much of the sorting has occurred spontaneously. Your close friends already know you're in recovery and have expressed interest in remaining a meaningful part of your life. Use these exercises to help you respond to friendships where reconnection is not happening naturally, where you need a little help in sorting out or reapproaching each other.

Questions: Is there anyone you want to tell about your recovery whom you have not yet contacted? Who? Why?

_____

_____

_____

Warning Signs and Signs of Support

There is a difference between the discomfort of establishing new boundaries between trusted friends and the discomfort of not being able to communicate your needs because the trust is gone. Both situations may tie your stomach in a knot and set off a barrage of negative self-talk, but in a situation where redefinition is likely to work, a little voice and a little light will break through and inform you that what you want is still possible.

> For weeks I avoided an old friend because I was sure when I told him that I had spent my summer vacation in treatment instead of hiking in the Rockies like I said I had, he would throw me away. In my mind, I kept imagining him being angry, accusing me of lying, acting hurt that I hadn't

taken him into my confidence. At least as long as I didn't really talk to him, I could tell myself I still had one friend. Finally, he cornered me, arrived at my house one evening with pizza and mineral water. It was almost a signal that he already knew because we had always had a six-pack of beer on pizza nights. When I told him the truth, he cried before I did and said how sad he was to think of the pain I must have been in.

Sometimes your anxiety is valid.

I called a friend I really trusted and told him I wasn't going to drink anymore and wanted to find things we could do together that didn't involve alcohol. My "friend" spent twenty minutes on the phone trying to convince me that my drinking didn't seem that bad to him and he didn't think I was really an alcoholic. I couldn't get him to listen, so I finally just had to hang up. It really shook me and shook loose all the voices in my own mind that argue about how to define myself. Christ, when you're new to recovery, saying, "I'm an alcoholic," is hard enough without having a long-time friend tell you, "No, you're not."

To help you tell the difference and decide what you need to do with the friends you already have, thinking about the following questions and examples may be useful in assessing who is supportive and who is not. If you feel uncertain about a particular friend, go through this section, see which example seems closest to your situation (even if the language doesn't exactly match how you and your friends speak), and try to answer the questions as honestly as you can.

One of the changes occurring in recovery is that you are learning a new way of speaking about yourself, your history, your feelings, your needs and wants in relationship to other people. And you are challenging other people who are important to you to speak about themselves and their view of the relationship differently also.

This change in patterns of communication may at first seem very strange—like learning a foreign language while still speaking English. The sentences and syntax may not feel natural to you. You may be thinking, "My friends and I don't talk like that . . . I'm not even sure I *want* to talk like that . . ." You will discover your own way of communicating. You don't need to adopt the methods used in this book word for word; take what fits and practice with it.

Questions: Does your friend listen without defining or judging who you are and what your problem is? How do you know? (What does s/he say and do that helps you feel accepted or judged in his/her eyes?)

_____

_____

_____

Sample warning-sign statement: *"I never saw you overeat. Why do you have to make such a big deal about being a little overweight? Almost everybody carries around an extra ten pounds."*

Sample support statement: *"I'm sorry that you've had to struggle with this alone. How can I help? Will you tell me if I make insensitive statements or ask you to do something that makes you uncomfortable?"*

Questions: In what ways do you feel accepted? judged?

_____

_____

_____

Sample warning-sign statement: *"I don't know—I don't think of my friends as alkies. I suppose this means you're going to those meetings where everybody sits around and talks about how great it was to be a drunk—now that you can't drink."*

Sample support statement: *"It takes courage to go through this and I know you're going to change. But you'll always be my good 'ole friend' too."*

Questions: Do your friend's challenges feel supportive? How and how not?

_____

_____

_____

Sample warning-sign statement: *"You shouldn't feel so down on your parents; they're only trying to help. It's a pretty big shock to them, too, that suddenly you've decided your whole family is dysfunctional and hauled them into family group therapy."*

Sample support statement: *"I wonder if you're being realistic about giving up alcohol, cigarettes, and sugar all at once. Is there some way you could make these changes and still be gentle with yourself?"*

In your new patterns of friendship, a healthy repartee can develop. You accept challenges and you offer challenges. You accept support and you offer support. This may not have worked very well in the past, but the above support statements offer models for the kinds of mutual exchange possible when both friends are contributing to the work and play of friendship.

Clearing up communication patterns is part of acting "as if." When you act "as if," you do something that seems foreign until you have made it your own. If you've never hit a tennis ball before, it will seem like a foreign activity. You have to move your body in ways that feel very "unnatural," but it works. These strange movements send the ball in the direction you want, and gradually the movements become natural, a kind of dance. Abstinence is foreign behavior, but in the early stages of recovery, you act as if abstinence is natural. This attitude enables you to grow into it. Speaking as directly to your friends as outlined here, and in upcoming chapters, may also seem very foreign. You can remain true to your personality and your own style, and practice making changes in communication which will allow your friendships to develop very differently than they did in the past.

Saying Good-bye to Friends You Cannot Keep

You might need to see certain people from your past in order to make amends, to let them know about your addiction and recovery, or to terminate the relationship because it poses a threat to your recovery.

There *are* times when warning bells should go off. And you've already thought about some of these instances in the previous section. When you are newly recovering and among old friends, you have a responsibility to avoid people who jeopardize your recovery. You know best what threatens your recovery and abstinence. "Being friends" does not mean calling up old drinking buddies and practicing keeping boundaries over a few beers or going to an all-you-can-eat buffet to "bond" with someone if you are recovering from an eating disorder or going to the horse races with friends from your gambling past.

Question: How might you allow someone to pose a threat to your recovery?

_____

_____

_____

Question: What steps could you take now to protect yourself?

_____

_____

_____

Growing apart is one of the bittersweet aspects of recovery and of life in general. The friend who used to canvass liberal causes with you may have become a conservative. Your old jogging partner is into swimming. That's okay. People change and the changes aren't always parallel. There are over five billion people on the planet, plenty of potential friends to choose from.

Taking a Friendship Inventory

If you feel that it is necessary or desirable to move beyond a particular friendship, you may want to take an inventory of the friendship to determine why you don't think it will work anymore. As those of you in Twelve Step programs discovered when you began taking your own personal inventory in Step Four, a good inventory includes both assets and liabilities. Taking a balanced view of a friendship can help you decide what action is most appropriate. Asking yourself specific questions might help you inventory your friendship. For instance :

• Does this friendship jeopardize your recovery? How?

_____

_____

• Are there still benefits that you derive from this friendship? Is it safe to stay in the friendship to reap those benefits? (Yes or no and why?)

_____

_____

• Do you and your friend practice mutual respect? How?

_____

_____

• How does your friend help you grow in ways conducive to your recovery? How do you contribute to your friend's growth?

_____

_____

• What interests do you and your friend still have in common?

_____

_____

- How do your differences enhance or inhibit your growth?

_____

_____

How you say good-bye to friends you cannot keep depends on the degree of closeness you had established and the kind of friendship you had in the first place. Ways of ending friendships might include no contact, indirect contact, or personal contact.

No Contact

Terminating some relationships might require no action on your part. Casual friends with whom you have had little or no recent contact over the years do not have to be told the friendship is over. If neither of you is initiating contact, the life span of the friendship has probably run its natural course. It is common for people to drift apart, and the distancing has probably been mutual, requiring no explanation on either friend's part.

> Bill and I used to hang out together before I went into treatment. We played pool a couple of times, stuff like that, but you wouldn't really call us close. We kind of lost touch, which feels okay. If we run into each other, we say hello, but we don't call each other anymore.

Unless one of you is being persistent or pushy, or unless you feel you need some sort of closure, you may also want to distance yourself silently from those people with whom you were bound together by drug or alcohol use or other addictive practices.

Indirect Contact

You may want to say good-bye to a friend in a letter in which you express how you feel but to which you do not seek an answer. Such a letter might read:

> Dear _____ ,
>   As you probably have heard, I've been in treatment for chemical dependency and am now in recovery. Recovery is changing how I feel about a lot of things, and I'm doing a lot of sorting. Our friendship gave me many good things, but I don't know how to continue with it. I feel the need to ask that we go our separate ways. Thank you for being part of my life. I wish you well.

Read your letter over, circle any "you's" in the letter and see if there is a way to change the statement to an "I," taking responsibility for only *your own* thoughts, feelings, and actions. If it is only one or two abrupt sentences, consider adding a little softness. If it is long and explanatory, consider editing it until you are sure your message is clear.

It may take several attempts to state clearly what you need to say. Short, direct, nonblaming sentences and a clear conclusion will best accomplish this type of termination. There is no need to punish yourself or your past friend. In life, we learn from all those with whom we interact in any significant way. It may be helpful and healing to stop and think about what you got and what you gave in the course of this friendship, to hold the good things in your mind as you say good-bye.

Whatever way you choose to say good-bye, remember that you can't script your friend's response or be sure how s/he will react to your leave-taking. If the plan for an accepting separation doesn't go as you anticipated, it does not mean you've failed. Do the best you can for yourself and for your recovery. These decisions get made both ways in life: sometimes you will be the one doing the leaving and sometimes you will be the one being left.

Direct Contact

You might also choose to say good-bye to a friend through a telephone call or in a personal meeting. This is the most challenging way to end a relationship, but it may feel necessary in certain circumstances. Your role is to be honest and willing to accept responsibility for what *you* think and feel and how *you* act and react. Whatever happens, your most important job is to protect your recovery above all else.

> I used to meet Marge at a downtown bar for happy hour at least three times a week after work. When I admitted I had a drinking problem and went into treatment, Marge tried to be supportive, but she still thought we should be able to meet at our old hangout. Without alcohol, I guess we didn't have much in common. I worked up the courage to meet Marge for coffee and told her I didn't think we could continue our friendship. She got furious, accused me of rejecting her, and stomped out of the coffee shop. I cried and cried and then called a program friend. I knew I did what I had to do, but it still felt rotten.

Dealing with anger and rejection—your own *or* your friend's—can make you feel vulnerable and can threaten your abstinence. Because you cannot predict how a friend will react to your saying good-bye, it is wise to have safeguards in place, such as calling a group member or sponsor. You may want to write down what you want to tell your friend in a dialogue, playing both roles and preparing yourself for several outcomes. Answering the following questions can also help you prepare for your encounter with your friend.

- What is the essential message you need to convey?

_____

_____

_____

- How will you react to a negative response?

_____

_____

_____

- How will you react to a supportive response?

_____

_____

_____

- If s/he supports you, do you intend to change your mind about ending the friendship? What new boundaries will you need to establish if you decide to maintain the friendship?

_____

_____

_____

• What are the good things you got from this friendship that you need to acknowledge?

_____

_____

_____

After answering these questions and writing out potential dialogues, you may want to role-play the scene with a friend. Take the role of your friend as well as practicing your own part. There's an old saying that in order to understand each other, we need to walk a mile in each other's shoes. Before you see your friend, walk in his or her shoes by writing dialogues and role playing. This is the practice of empathy.

Recovering People Can Change Their Minds

Recovery is a process that lasts a lifetime. What you decide today might not be your decision next week or ten years from now.

You might discover that after you express your concerns to your friend and relate your need for distance, your friend responds with a willingness to support your recovery and a desire to work hard to continue the relationship. You have the right to reconsider and continue the friendship *and* you have the right to stick to your guns and leave even if your friend pleads with you to stay. If you make one decision now, you can change your mind when it feels comfortable to do so. Of course, during this time, your friend also has the right and the opportunity to change his/her mind.

I tried to end this one friendship four times before I finally called it quits. My friend kept making these convincing arguments why we should still be friends. The friendship was not good for either of us—we brought out the worst of our codependent characteristics with each other. I feel a little sad it's over, but mainly I just feel this overwhelming sense of relief.

———————

I kept trying to leave Karen because I knew we were really enmeshed, but in spite of all our confusion we also really loved each other. We kept wanting to do the best thing for each other—so, I'd back away, then she'd back away. But one of us would always call the other. It was obvious that we wanted to be friends, but we both knew the kind of relationship we had wasn't good for either of us. We decided to go to a couple of therapy sessions together, and each of us joined an Al-Anon group. Our friendship feels really balanced now. I'm glad we trusted each other enough to hang in there.

4

Making
New Friends

As new and healthier habits replace old ones and recovery becomes a more usual part of your everyday living, you won't feel
the need to focus as much of your attention on maintaining
recovery itself. Recovery steadily becomes an integrated aspect of
how you conduct your life. This integration allows you to be
curious about other things, to have a basic sense of confidence in
the changes you are making, and to muster the courage to explore
the world around you. Curiosity, courage, and confidence are
important ingredients for making new friends.

In *Restore Your Life*, Dr. Anne Geller cautions newly recovering
people:

A good rule to follow for friendships in early sobriety is that
less is often more. This applies to quantity as well as to
quality. You'll benefit much more from a few good friends,
old or new, who can encourage you in sobriety, than from an

extensive social network in which you have no one to whom you can talk candidly.[1]

The first place you meet new people in recovery is at group meetings. Then as you become more involved in new activities and interests, you will probably meet friends outside of self-help groups.

Is Fellowship Friendship?

There is an honesty, a shared intimacy, and a level of acceptance between members of a support group that is difficult to replicate, but does this constitute friendship? When friendship is a free and equal bond of mutual respect that encourages healthy growth and accepts individuality, does this fit the model for the support group experience? The answer is an ambiguous one: a shared experience can be the basis for a close and long-lasting friendship, but mutual recovery goals alone do not ensure friendship. Some people have met their best friends at self-help meetings, while others choose not to socialize with group members.

Once a week or so, people in a self-help setting engage in a kind of communion with others who, like themselves, struggle to recover. As the saying goes, "there are no strangers here, only friends we have not met."

I can still remember my first Twelve Step meeting. I stayed in my car till the last minute and almost didn't go in. When the meeting started and we joined hands to say the Serenity Prayer, I wanted to bolt, it felt so weird. At the end of it, when we held hands again and everybody said, "Keep coming back. It works," there was something going on that made me believe them. After a few more meetings, these people—even though I didn't know them very well—felt like friends. They were nonjudgmental and accepting. They didn't care about my mistakes; they cared about whether or not I was honest about wanting to get better.

Trust and the Anonymity Factor

The agreement to respect and preserve the anonymity of individuals and not disclose the intimacies exchanged is a basic trust in recovery and support groups. Because of this, members need to be cautious when they strike up friendships outside the meeting. As one Al-Anon member put it, "Those four walls hold a lot during meetings. I like to keep it there within them."

Self-help group participants are frequently reminded that what is said at a meeting stays at the meeting.

I go to an AA meeting in my neighborhood. One night a guy I know from church started coming to the same meeting. At first, it felt awkward because we knew each other in such a different context and know so many of the same people. We've had to work on keeping these two things separate. We agreed, at least for the time being, not to talk about AA outside our AA meeting.

It is easy to blur boundaries in situations like the one described above. These men were successful in negotiating boundaries because they acknowledged their discomfort and, together, agreed upon standards of behavior that would allow them to participate fully in their AA group while protecting their anonymity outside of meetings.

Questions: Is there anyone in your recovery group that you know in another context? Are your boundaries for associating outside of meetings clear? If not, what can you do to clarify them?

_____

_____

_____

If you decide to pursue a relationship formed in a recovery group, you know that both of you share a common commitment and have a similar spiritual framework; but you also share a commitment to respect and preserve the anonymity of other members. There are boundary issues implicit in any friendship that develops outside of meetings. Here are some guidelines:

- Don't use stories or events from your meeting as the starting point of conversations, unless you are referring to your own contributions.
- Don't gossip about other members or former members.
- If you break confidentiality ("Besides our ACOA meeting, Betty goes to AA too, you know . . .") stop, catch yourself, say "oops," and start the conversation over in another direction.
- Find other things you have in common besides recovery: children, work, hobbies, etc.
- Find things you like to *do* together, not just talk.

Striking a Balance: Taking Friendships Beyond Your Group Meetings

Discovering individuals who spark your interest and stimulate your growth is always a gift. When you share the journey of recovery, you provide each other with an added level of understanding—or *misunderstanding*. If you want to take a friendship beyond the experience of recovery meetings, the following tips offered by people who have created such friendships may help:

73

• **Take It Slowly.** Chat with a potential friend before or after a meeting. Talk about movies, hobbies, sports, politics, etc. Notice your comfort level *and* theirs. Do they seem to want to know more about you? If so, suggest going out for coffee after a meeting or talking a walk. Set up a fairly brief time span, so if it doesn't work neither of you gets uncomfortable.

• **Make a Conscious Decision Not to Discuss Other Group Members.** Keeping each other on track in this regard will build trust. If you notice each other being respectful of people who aren't there, it reassures you that you will be respected in absence also. Of course, what you discuss that pertains to the two of you is up to the two of you.

• **Do Not Let Your Friendship Interfere with the Work at Group Meetings.** Sometimes cliques develop within larger groups. Such cliques and alliances can cause resentment and impede group process. Practice being inclusive. Do not exclude newcomers and others at your meetings.

• **Keep Your Expectations Reasonable.** This budding friendship may not work. As you begin exploring conversational topics and interests, you may discover that, apart from group meetings, you have very little in common. When this happens, accept it as a natural part of life. If you've gone slowly, and neither of you has overinvested emotionally, it will be easy to go back to an in-group relationship where you can concentrate on the one thing you know for sure you share: your commitment to recovery.

Questions: Is there anyone in your support group you would like to get to know better, outside of meetings? Why do you think you want to know them?

_____

_____

_____

Getting to Know a Group Member Better

Sometimes it can be awkward to try out new ways of approaching others, or letting yourself be approached. The discomfort that accompanies a new behavior doesn't necessarily mean something is wrong, only that you are doing something or reacting to someone differently.

If you are used to enmeshed relationships, the following guidelines may seem too short and lacking explanation. If you are used to disengaged relationships, the guidelines may seem too direct or intimate. Middle ground is new territory for almost everyone. You are practicing being a social person—not practicing perfection.

• If you want to extend an invitation to coffee after a meeting, be clear and specific in your request, rather than open-ended and vague. Say something like:

I really liked what you had to say about the Step tonight. It got me thinking about a lot of things that have happened in my own life. Would you like to join me now for a cup of coffee?

• Saying something like "We should get together sometime," does not really communicate your sincerity and might be interpreted as mere politeness. If a group member approaches you to go out for coffee and you would really like to go, ask for clarification or specifics. Say something like:

That sounds fun. I usually have some time on meeting nights before I need to get home. Do you mean tonight or next week?

• After you've been out together, you may want to think about the following questions. How did your time together go? Did you feel comfortable with the person? Were you interested in what s/he had to say and did you want to learn more? Were you enthused about sharing your own thoughts and stories? Did anything make you uncomfortable? Did s/he seem to feel comfortable with you? Would you like to see this person again? Did you exchange phone numbers or make plans to get together again?

If you were not comfortable, it would be helpful to understand why. Did you get scared being asked to reveal yourself? Is this just a reaction to your being strangers? If so, do you think you could tolerate your own or the other person's discomfort? Did s/he do something that changed your mind about wanting to get to know him/her? What?

If you are not interested in getting together again, the other person may not be interested either. Discomfort is often a shared experience. However, if you are given another invitation and you don't want to pursue a friendship, you need to be ready to decline.

There's a popular T-shirt emblazoned with the question, "What part of the word NO don't you understand?" It is very difficult sometimes simply to say no, but it is also an important practice in your recovery. "No, thank you" is a way of showing respect for yourself and for others. There will be times when you need the courage to say it, and times when you need the graciousness to hear it. No explanation is necessary.

If you decide you do want to explore the possibility of friendship, note any things that could make the next visit more comfortable. For example, what are the boundary issues that need to be looked at?

One night after an ACOA meeting, another guy and I decided to go out for coffee and dessert. We really hit it off. Both his parents were alcoholics like mine; he was married and has kids like me—our lives and experiences were very similar. We're going to get together again and even talked about our families getting together. When I got home, though, it hit me how easy it had been to give each other advice. We got into solving each other's problems pretty fast! I think we'll have to talk about that next time we see each other. Feels like we need some guidelines or we might end up running each other's lives instead of our own.

The Choice Is Yours

Recovery is a process of making responsible choices. There are no rules that say you have to socialize with people at your support group meetings or make friends with them, even if they indicate a willingness or desire to develop a friendship outside of meetings. *You* choose.

> In Al-Anon, a lot of people go out to a local café after each meeting for coffee. They invited me, and I knew it was sort of an honor to be asked, but I never went. I didn't want to end up being asked about my work or my lover. I liked the anonymity of the group, being just another person with a first name only and a family member who had trouble with alcohol. I tell the truth in our Step discussions, but that's different than socializing.

It's also okay not to be quite sure *how* you feel about making friends with group members. It is natural throughout recovery (and throughout life) to struggle with boundary issues. If you discovered in Chapter 2 that you have a tendency to become enmeshed in a relationship, you might be afraid that you could get too involved in your new friend's life. If you have a tendency to be disengaged, you might be afraid a new friend would want more from the relationship than you feel comfortable offering.

If you're struggling with ambivalence about a potential group friend, review Chapter 2 and write down your thoughts to explore why you are feeling uncertain. It may be useful to make a line down the middle of a page and write two lists.

Why I'm interested in becoming friends with X	Why I'm hesitant to become friends with X
_____	_____
_____	_____
_____	_____
_____	_____

Whatever you do or decide not to do, be easy with yourself and take it slowly. Asking a person out for coffee does not mean you'll have to be a godparent to his or her child. And refusing a cup of coffee does not mean you can never become friends.

So far, I've chosen not to encourage friendships at OA [Overeaters Anonymous]. For me, it has to do with my obsessive/compulsive tendencies. Part of my recovery is learning not to think about food or dwell on the behavior which brings me there in the first place. I feel comfortable contacting a member when I need to or having someone call me if they need to. I try to be conscious of balance and boundaries. I have to watch myself or I take on other people's pain. For me, at this stage in my recovery, my meetings are a respite in my life, a place where I go for sustenance, and I don't want social expectations to develop in this protected place.

Whether or not you choose to socialize with people at your meetings, you will discover that fellow members are a constant source of support whose understanding serves you when you need them most.

I attend two different Twelve Step meetings. I hadn't been going very long when my dad died. I called up one person from each group and was totally amazed at the outpouring of sympathy and support these folks gave me. At the wake, my aunt noticed all the supportive "strangers" around me and then whispered, "I never realized having a disease could be so beneficial!"

Making Friends Within the Larger Recovery Community

When Bill W. founded Alcoholics Anonymous over half a century ago, there was nothing else like it in the world. If you wanted to make friends with someone who really understood you and who supported your recovery, AA was your single option.

Thanks to the tremendous success and acceptance of Alcoholics Anonymous and other Twelve Step programs, you don't have to search very far to meet someone in a recovery program. Today, concepts and practices of recovery and personal growth are common in many people's lives. Acceptance has grown to such an extent that recovering people can find friends outside of their own meeting who will honor and encourage their commitment to recovery. Al-Anon members are friends with Adult Children of Alcoholics (ACOA) who are friends with members of Emotions Anonymous who are friends with AA members. Every state has an annual Roundup, and Intergroup meetings are held in most larger towns and cities. What Bill W. set in motion is like a nuclear reaction with positive shock waves continuing to extend out from the AA core.

Although I don't get together socially with members of my own Codependents Anonymous group, many of my friends are in other Twelve Step groups. Talking to them adds new and different dimensions to my recovery.

And Now a Word from (and for) Our Sponsors

Newcomers to Twelve Step programs are encouraged to choose a longtime member to act as a sponsor. A sponsor is a guide— someone who has been abstinent (or active in Al-Anon and codependency recovery) for at least one year. The purpose of the sponsor is to give you a personal mentor with whom you can discuss topics not covered at meetings. A sponsor is someone you can call when you feel shaky or overwhelmed or when you simply need someone to talk to.

A good sponsor/sponsee relationship contains the elements of friendship: honesty, trust, mutual respect, and acceptance. There *is* a difference, however. A sponsor agrees that you may call him/her for information, reassurance, emergency support—but the sponsor doesn't call you to get those things. If s/he needs to, s/he calls her/his sponsor. There is mutuality, but not mutual dependence. And that significantly changes the definition of the relationship. There are sponsors and there are friends. Each comes into your life differently. A sponsor may be friendly and may become a friend, but the initial connection does not have the balance of friendship.

The sponsor is a mentor, not a buddy. A sponsor has assumed this role *because* s/he has experience working in the program and can guide you.

My sponsor is a very important part of my life. However, we do not do things socially together. He is helping me work the Steps, figure out my food plan, helping me get rid of secrets. This feels more important than going to a movie with him.

One of the benefits of sponsoring someone else's recovery is that it helps the sponsor work a better program too.

I am a sponsor, even though I'm an awkward one at times. I have no specific guidelines that I follow other than listening and offering encouragement when it is sought. The boundaries for sponsorship are laid out in the practice of the Twelve Steps, and I follow those.

Friendship is based on mutual exchange. You and your sponsor have other areas of equality and mutuality; you may even be older or more experienced in other aspects of living, but the sponsor/sponsee relationship is set up *intentionally* to be unequal in order to provide you with safety and security.

While a friend may tell you what you want to hear, an effective sponsor tells you what you *need* to hear in order to maintain abstinence. This doesn't mean that a sponsor steps in and runs your life.

Questions: What role does your sponsor play in your recovery program? (Or, if you don't yet have a sponsor, what role do you think a sponsor should play in your recovery?)

_____

_____

_____

Choosing a Sponsor

We are usually drawn to people who are like us, who share our ideas, values, likes, and dislikes. But do not look for a twin when you choose a sponsor. Seek guidance or role modeling from a sponsor but try not to replace your own friends (or lack of them) with this person. Friendship grows mutually; it isn't created to fit a prearranged structure.

You get a sponsor in order to keep *your* recovery on track, so you need an accessible sponsor—someone who will be available to answer your questions or hear your program concerns. Find someone who has time, someone who will be direct and who is making personal progress. Pick someone whose recovery is a model for the kind of recovery you want.

Some of the most successful sponsor/sponsee relationships bring together very different people. A sponsor who offers a different perspective can be valuable in helping you find new and creative solutions to your problems. You and your sponsor can be as different as night and day; the only thing you need to share is a sincere desire to recover and gain the wholeness that recovery brings.

When I first started going to Narcotics Anonymous, I found myself attracted to people who looked and sounded like me. I was tempted to ask one of them to sponsor me, but held off for a few meetings. One night, the topic was sponsorship and a guy related an experience of getting a sponsor too much like himself. He said that for months they got nowhere because his sponsor kept saying, "I know just what you mean. I do that too." Instead of guidance, he got empathy. It got me thinking. I've got long hair and play in a rock band, but I ended up asking this investment

banker to sponsor me. It's a pretty weird combination, but he sure helps me work my program!

Listen carefully to people at your meetings. Watch how they act, react, and interact with others. See how they work their own program. It is generally recommended that sponsors and sponsees be of the same gender. Asking yourself the following questions might help you choose a sponsor:

- What qualities or traits does the prospective sponsor have that you think you want in terms of recovery?
- Has this person been working his or her program consistently for over a year?
- Does this person contribute honestly at meetings without pretending to have all the answers?
- Does this person listen attentively at meetings?
- Does this person attend meetings regularly?
- Are you comfortable talking privately with this person?
- Can you imagine asking him/her for help?
- Can you imagine being vulnerable with this person?
- Does this person have time to sponsor you?

If you answered yes to most of those questions, work up the courage and simply ask the prospect if s/he would be willing to sponsor you. If the answer is no, do not take it as a personal rejection; be thankful for the candid answer. It is better for a prospective sponsor to decline at the outset rather than make a commitment that s/he cannot fulfill. Look around, go through the checklist again, and ask someone else. Remember, it is perfectly fine to have more than one sponsor.

If there is no one in your group who can sponsor you or no one you care to approach right now, inquire at your local central office for a list of willing sponsors. It is common—especially when working the Fourth and Fifth Steps—to find a sponsor who doesn't attend your own Twelve Step meeting.

Sometimes recovering people decline to sponsor a newcomer because they are afraid they won't be the *perfect* sponsor. This shouldn't really surprise us, since perfectionism is a first cousin to addictive behavior. Sponsors are fallible human beings, just like everyone else. So you need to discuss what reasonable expectations each of you has in mind. This is good practice, because someday you may be asked to be a sponsor too.

Question: What do you want from a sponsor?

_____

_____

_____

The more clearly you state what you are looking for, the more clearly a prospective sponsor can assess his/her ability to provide what you want. Both of you are seeking a healthy, workable match within the structures provided by the Twelve Steps.

Remember that your sponsor is not your parent. It is not your sponsor's job to feed, clothe, employ, or monetarily support you. It is not your sponsor's job to keep you abstinent; that is *your* responsibility. It *is* your sponsor's job to be truthful, to be supportive and accepting, and to be available to help you explore ways in which you might best work your program.

Some sponsors may want to define boundaries early on, or you may want to suggest certain guidelines that might make the relationship a smooth-working one. For instance, certain hours for telephoning might be set (unless, of course, an emergency arises) or you might agree that neither of you wants to receive calls at work. Communicating these simple guidelines can prevent misunderstanding, thwart arguments at home, and avoid resentments that might otherwise arise.

Question: What boundaries do you want to set or discuss with a sponsor?

_____

_____

_____

What to Do If a Sponsorship Doesn't Work Out

Some sponsorships don't work out. It is important for both the sponsor and the sponsee to realize that either one can ask to break the sponsoring relationship. If you decide that your sponsor isn't able to provide the guidance you need, be honest. If you can't work things out, release each other from the relationship with respect and gratitude because each of you cared enough to try.

Sometimes a sponsor does not remain abstinent. If this happens, it's a sign that the sponsor needs to take a break from being a sponsor and get his or her own recovery back on track.

> When I lost my abstinence, I told my sponsee that, for the time being, I could not act as a sponsor, that I had to concentrate exclusively on my own program. He seemed so disappointed, like I had really let him down, but I needed to be honest.

During incidents like this, it is extremely important to sort out your own issues from your sponsor's issues and to reinforce the fact that you are in charge of yourself and your own recovery. Recovery is a process in which we learn to move beyond shaming and blaming ourselves or others. If your sponsor has a slip, it is his or her slip, and it is his or her recovery that is in jeopardy. A slip has nothing to do with you; it was not an intentional act meant to hurt you or undermine your recovery. Of course you might feel confused, disappointed, worried, and concerned, but this wasn't something that happened to *you*. You and your sponsor are different people with different paths through recovery.

> When my sponsor said she'd slipped, I felt like I had slipped too. I began to question everything she'd ever told me. Then I went to a different meeting just to talk about it. These people advised me that, for the time being, I should not expect her to act as a sponsor and they offered to provide sponsorship.

The road to recovery is not always straight or smooth and no one can predict with certainty who will remain on course. You have no more control over your sponsor's actions than your sponsor has over your actions. Once you know this, you can support each other as two human beings in an imperfect process of growth.

Getting Ready to Leave the Nest

So far, most of this chapter, like most of your early recovery, has dealt with activities and people in recovery groups. But, as you are discovering, the world outside of your recovery network continues to exist. The longer and stronger you are in recovery, the more time and energy you will have to explore other interests.

As Dr. Anne Geller points out in *Restore Your Life*:

As you move beyond the first year of sobriety, it becomes easier to make friends outside the recovery network. Your recovery is well on its way to being an integral part of who you are and so it becomes possible to form new friendships based on common interests. . . . In the long run, the experience, strength, and hope you gain from your recovery will help you not only to make new friends, but also to be a better friend to everyone with whom you share the bond of friendship.[2]

Recovering people are often amazed at how time-consuming their addiction was, at how many hours were devoted to drinking, taking drugs, looking for drugs or alcohol, thinking about or practicing compulsive behavior.

When I stopped drinking, I found myself with a lot of free time, especially during football season. Before I went into treatment, I used to meet my buddies at our local hangout and we'd watch a game—any game that was on the tube that day—and get loaded.

Take a minute or two to think about today. If today was full, think about yesterday or last week.

Questions: Were there blocks of time when you found yourself with nothing to do? Were there moments when you would have liked to have shared an activity or experience with someone else? What would you have liked to do?

_____

_____

_____

Question: What is the most opportune time for you to pursue making new friends?

_____

_____

_____

After you've thought about the best times to meet new people and maybe try new activities, think about what you enjoy doing. What are your special interests? What are your passions?

Exercise: Make a list of the things you like doing or would like to learn. Just do this off the top of your head and be as inclusive as you can. Don't censor yourself or eliminate something because you don't have the skills or money. Include the following in your list:

- Favorite activities
- Things you would like to learn to do
- Things you can't imagine yourself doing but would like to try
- Things you've always wanted to be
- Places you've always wanted to go
- The types of people you've always wanted to know
- Times you feel best about yourself

Now take a few minutes to look over your lists. Put an asterisk (*) by your passions—the things you *really* love to do or really want to learn to do. Since this book is about recovery and friendship, the only rules here are that the activities should include other people and should in no way jeopardize your recovery. If you are recovering from an eating disorder, it is not wise to focus on food or make food central to your activity choice. If you are a recovering alcoholic, you might not want to engage in things that previously highlighted drinking. Since the purpose of this exercise is to identify possible ways to connect with others, concentrate on social activities from your list. Although you may continue to enjoy two-hour baths, you are not likely to meet new friends in your tub!

Brainstorm on your restructured list. Get creative. Note where you might find a group, a class, or an opportunity that offers what you're looking for. For instance, local community education offices or the YMCA/YWCA might have information on a walking club. Many cities have telephone information referral services. Local librarians are also good resources.

Working a recovery program can get serious and exhausting. It's necessary to take a break from soul-searching and concentrate on new activities. When we do this, we find that these endeavors are not side trips, but an integral part of recovery.

Questions: What new activity are you willing to pursue this week? How will you go about pursuing it?

_____

_____

_____

Volunteering Friendships

Part of recovery is learning how to be less obsessed with yourself, a chemical, or certain types of behavior. Volunteering is a worthwhile way to try out skills while providing much-needed services. People can benefit from your presence and you can benefit from their presence. Helping others is also an excellent way to keep your recovery on track and to make amends for past actions or wrongdoings. If you've harmed someone in the past but cannot make amends because doing so would hurt that person more, doing a good deed for someone else helps you forgive yourself.

> When I was a heavy into drugs, I used to steal money from the lady who lived downstairs in my apartment building. She died before I could tell her how sorry I was or pay her back. About six months ago, I began doing some volunteer work for a local food shelf. One day when I was there packing up food and giving it out, an image of my neighbor lady popped into my brain as clear as anything. Somehow, I felt like she forgave me. It's strange. I didn't start working there thinking I was doing penance or anything. Someone in my group said I experienced a moment of grace.

There are many things you can do as a volunteer. Literacy projects need tutors, the blind need readers, community agencies need office workers and consultants. Schools and churches always need help.

Look in the Yellow Pages, call information or contact your county information office to find the number of your local voluntary action program or local volunteer coordinator. Being of service is one way to practice skills and reintroduce yourself to the world. Volunteering can build confidence that carries you back to a more personal arena of friendship. However, be realistic about the time, commitment, and energy required. You still need to take good care of yourself. Remember to stay your own best friend.

5

Greeting Strangers and Making Them Friends

Many people rebel at the idea that any relationship, but especially friendship, *ought* to require conscious planning, ground rules, and negotiated guidelines. Somehow we hope that the person we choose as a friend will automatically tune into our needs so that the relationship and will effortlessly and spontaneously fulfill our heart's desires.

To succeed in friendship, we need to give up these notions of magic compatibility and replace them with a willingness to be straightforward, direct, and simple in what we ask for and what we offer. For example, an exchange such as the following one lays good groundwork for friendship, no matter what these two women decide to do:

There was a woman in my Step group who wanted to be my friend. It seemed that every time I opened my mouth, she'd say, "Oh, I know just what you mean." One night I snapped

at her, "No you don't." She looked really hurt and surprised. At the next meeting, I told her "I think it made me
so mad to hear you say that because I used to say it all the
time. Want to have coffee and figure out what we can both
do differently?" Once we began talking about what we
really had in common, we stopped irritating each other.
Maybe we will become friends.

One of the realities of recovery is the need to practice making
ourselves aware of the thoughts, feelings, and beliefs that drive
our lives. This need to become more aware also exists when we
look at friendship in recovery.

I never understood why certain kids liked me or didn't like
me in school. I was just grateful to be included. When I
grew up and looked for friends at work or in the neighborhood, the process of liking someone or being liked stayed
just as mysterious. Whenever somebody liked me, I
thought it meant we had all kinds of things in common and
that they were interested in taking care of me. I didn't know
this until years later working my ACOA [Adult Children of
Alcoholics] program, but I was like walking Swiss cheese, a
person full of holes that I expected friends to fill.

You need to be aware what your fantasy about friendship is.
You won't become aware all at once, but each excursion into
friendly interaction will teach you valuable lessons and provide
many insights. As long as you and your friends are willing to
accept friendship as a growing, changing experiment, and look
back at your histories with a sense of humor as well as respect, the
process of learning doesn't have to be painful.

Laying a Good Groundwork for Friendship

The groundwork for friendship is laid by our willingness to take chances, to risk offering ourselves to another person, and to accept what they have to offer. To practice friendship, we take chances: Sometimes our interest won't be returned, or our expectations won't be met exactly as we hoped and we'll get our feelings hurt. This is normal. Human beings are clumsy, even when we're doing our best. We misread signals and don't know how to avoid each other's secret sore spots. We keep at it anyway because when connection works, it feels wonderful. We are infused with affection, excitement, a sense of belonging and being chosen. Friendship seems worth the chances we take and the vulnerability we experience.

When we practice friendship, we are constantly correcting our course. If you were flying a jet plane, the instrument panel would help you make constant, tiny, minute-by-minute corrections in altitude, direction, cabin pressure, etc. You wouldn't be a responsible pilot if you decided to wait until something was "really wrong"—like you'd fallen five hundred feet or an engine went out—before you mentioned or tried to correct a problem.

However, in relationships, we often let all the little things slide and build up resentment and misunderstanding until there is no way to correct the situation or until correction is difficult and painful. When we practice correcting our course with other people, interactions occur more often, more smoothly, and with less drama. When problems are small, consequences are small, and life goes on. In course correction, we state out loud what is happening between us as a statement of fact, and we find out what can be done to fix, correct, and resolve the problem.

In friendship, course correction can be subtle. We learn each other's signals, likes and dislikes, how to have fun together, what makes us laugh, and what we need to listen to in each other. We adjust our friendship naturally. When this spontaneous course correction doesn't work, we need to practice skills of being straightforward, direct, and simple. For example, when one friend's comment gets on another's nerves, course correction might look like this:

SAM: Must be rough, being a free-lance artist—no regular hours; working at home; sleeping in. Someday you ought to try a real job like the rest of us.

JO: You know, Sam, this is about the tenth time you've made cracks like that and it's starting to piss me off.

SAM: Hey, I'm kidding. Can't you take a joke?

JO: Well, it might have been funny at first, but it's getting kind of old and, to tell you the truth, it hurts my feelings. I feel like you don't think my work is as important as yours or something.

SAM: God, I'm sorry. I guess I'm sort of jealous—you seem to be doing what you really like and you get to call the shots. I didn't mean to hurt your feelings. I'm glad you told me.

Course correction is the practice of taking consistent small risks that keep you and your friend on track, building trust in your ability to be spontaneous and understood. It is not likely that Sam's comment about Jo's work will end their friendship—as long as both of them are willing to respond to each other and to grow in their sensitivity and appreciation of each other. If Jo stayed out of touch with her anger, and Sam stayed out of touch with his jealousy, however, these emotions could erode the friendship. By taking the risk to be direct, Jo and Sam build confidence in each other. They develop a track record of successful course correction.

This kind of risk-taking is a normal activity in friendship. Activity implies movement, change, the ability to be flexible. Whenever you interact, you practice skills of flexibility and response. In biological terms, response is a sign of life: the healthy organism is one capable of response. If you look at an amoeba under a microscope and poke at it with a tiny needle, the amoeba scuttles away. For an amoeba, this is a healthy reaction to irritation.

Human beings have been conditioned to ignore and deny the relationship between stimulus and response. We often don't know what is bothering us, what is pleasing us, who is being supportive, who is being disrespectful. Even as we become aware of these things, we may not know what reaction or response is appropriate. The only way to understand healthy response is to practice it. In friendship, social interaction is a nonphysiological way of practicing stimulus and response.

Question: What irritations did you learn *not* to respond to? (For example, if your father was drunk, it may have been dangerous to try to defend yourself, so you learned not to perceive or respond to anger at that level.)

_____

_____

_____

Question: What responses did you learn that don't seem to relate to the stimulus? (For example, you may notice you get sad when others get angry, or that you retreat when someone is trying to be friendly.)

_____

_____

_____

If you write out responses to these questions, you might write something like this:

Irritations I didn't respond to: 1. If I asked a question and nobody answered me, I didn't know I'd been ignored. 2. If someone was very angry, I didn't assume I had the right to defend myself. I just took whatever they dished out.

Breakdowns in stimulus/response: 1. If someone hurt my feelings I got depressed, and it took hours before I traced my drop in mood to something someone else said or did. And it took even longer before I understood how some belief I carried around added to my depression. 2. When someone criticized me I got ashamed instead of thinking about what they said.

Understanding our responses gives us a map of internal issues that we are likely to encounter in friendships. You have issues and your friend has issues and part of the bond between you becomes the willingness to help each other with the issues you bring to friendship.

My friend Jane really got shamed a lot as a kid. I've learned that I have to be really careful about how I bring up a problem—even my voice tone. If I can help us get through the place where she's likely to feel ashamed, I know we can deal with anything. My carefulness is teaching me a lot too.

We take risks and people take risks with us. We interact with and respond to each other and learn to think about the helpfulness, value, and appropriateness of our responses. Out of this ongoing process of risk and successful learning, trust is born. We become willing to be more and more vulnerable in front of and with each other. We become friends.

97

Learning to R.I.S.K.

Risk is the first activity in friendship. It begins when we say hello. To greet a stranger means taking risks—chancing rejection and disappointment. But taking risks also means opening ourselves up to new possibilities, new people, new adventures.

Before treatment, I think my closest friend was fear. I was afraid to live without drugs and I was afraid that drugs would kill me. I hid behind my fear—used it as an excuse. Now that I'm off drugs, my biggest fear is people. I'm afraid they won't like me or that I'll like somebody too much and end up getting hurt. My counselor says that I have to keep trying—get out there and meet new people. I know he's right, but it's still scary. Well, at least fear is familiar, gives me somebody to talk to in my head.

A popular saying in recovery groups is "Courage is fear that has said its prayers." When you face fear and use it to motivate your risk-taking, you change your relationship to this emotion. You turn fear into a positive and manageable experience. Most fear is fantasy ("Maybe they won't like me, maybe I'll be misunderstood"). There is no way to ascertain whether your fear is fantasy or reality without risking. Experience is real: Something happens. We can work with experience. We can develop ways to cope, talk to people about what happened, change our minds about its meaning. To say, "I tried this. Here's what happened. Here's what I don't understand. Here's what I want to do next . . ." is the great gift of experience. To acquire experience, we have to risk stepping out of fantasy into interaction.

By itself, the word *risk* may sound scary or negative. But if you take the word letter by letter and make an acronym out of it, RISK becomes a positive call to action:

R—Relax and enjoy the adventure
I— Imagine the possibilities
S— Surrender the need to control
K—Know that you are not alone

When you're getting ready to interact with someone for the first time, say to yourself, *"RISK it, RISK it,"* and remember your new definition. Relax, imagine, surrender, know.

But telling yourself to go ahead and risk it is a little like telling yourself to go ahead and recover. You may say, "I want to, but I don't know how. I don't know what you mean."

You practice recovery by

- Being abstinent
- Attending meetings
- Living one day at a time

You practice risking by

- Saying hello
- Paying attention equally to your reactions and to the other person's reactions
- Sharing something about yourself and creating dialogue

Saying Hello

Saying hello is a time-honored ritual that spans cultures and continents. A greeting is a signal that interaction has begun; initial contact has been established. In *Contact: The First Four Minutes,* Dr. Leonard Zunin contends that what happens in the first four minutes after greeting a person sets the tone for what happens next.[1] Zunin has observed that, in our culture, four minutes is the average time it takes for people to interact before they decide whether or not to continue the conversation or break away from it. He calls this phase of social encounter the hello phase.

Four minutes can feel like a very long or a very short period of time. Zunin's thesis is not meant to add pressure but to increase awareness. When we're "falling in love," that is, when a person strikes our romantic fancy, we know how to read the barometer of our interest and, hopefully, of the other person's interest. When we're looking for friendship, we may not even know that the same greeting behavior occurs.

> I met someone I really liked at a moment when I was confused about whether I wanted a friend or a lover. We didn't talk about sex, but I was throwing off a lot of sexual vibes. I think my new friend was unsure about me for a long time in a way she just couldn't name. So eventually I 'fessed up, told her what had happened and that I didn't want her to think I was still confused. She seemed really surprised, but her hesitance went away. She said, "If you're willing to risk telling me that, I know I can trust you to be honest about other things."

Contact is an automatic and highly intuitive function. We all do it, whether or not we are aware of it. We can use contact, and misuse it. In looking for friends, we need to use contact as wisely as we are able. You will not be perfect. You *will* learn from each encounter and be able to apply what you learn to the next encounter. If contact is mutually satisfying, you will have many opportunities to clarify your original connection.

Questions: Think of a very new person in your life. Have you connected? What were those first four minutes of contact like?

_____

_____

_____

Questions: How did this first encounter set the tone for your friendship? How have you changed and adjusted since then?

_____

_____

_____

I've known Ellen for eighteen years. We go out every year on the anniversary of our meeting and talk about what it was like to meet each other and how we've changed since then. I notice I'm doing that kind of reminiscing in several friendships now. It provides a kind of mental stability to tell the story of where we came from and how we met.

Zunin says that four elements are always present in a "good contact situation": confidence, creativity, caring, and consideration. These four C's are the essential sparks in making good contact. Everyone can recall contacts that were successful and those that were fraught with miscalculations.

I remember meeting Connie registering for writing class. Her energy was exciting and intriguing. I was swept in <u>and</u> intimidated, fearful I could not keep pace with her.

Do not use Zunin to add pressure to your risk-taking. As you say hello, the purpose of thinking about confidence, creativity, caring, and consideration is to increase your awareness of what messages you send and what you are receiving. If you listen carefully to the voice of intuition, it will help you get off to a good start.

> I remember hanging up the phone after Todd called to ask me directions to a bookstore I had mentioned—knowing she would be an important person in my life. I could hardly wait to begin our friendship.

The more honest you can be with yourself, the more honesty you will invite in others. If someone you have just met is likely to end up wanting things from you that you are uncomfortable offering, would you prefer to know it as you say hello or six months later? Contact is an invitation to awareness. Awareness is a good guide, even though it runs through the filter of our fantasies, our experience, and our secret hopes. Even though awareness is always filtered, it still helps us keep track of reality.

Questions: Is there anyone with whom you have made "good contact" recently whom you would like to see again? What is keeping you from calling this person? (If you decide that you want to see this person again, decide when you will call and what you will suggest doing together.)

_____

_____

_____

Paying Attention

The second element of risk-taking is paying equal attention to your own reactions and to the reactions of the other person. To pay attention means to develop a double focus: the ability to be aware of yourself—registering your own thoughts, feelings, and reactions—at the same time you are aware of how the other person is interacting with you and the signals s/he is sending.

You can't determine whether or not the other person might become a friend if you're so wrapped up in your own thoughts and feelings that you can hardly register their presence over the roar of your own self-criticism or self-congratulations. You also can't determine the possibility of friendship if you are so focused on them and their response you don't know how you feel about the interaction.

Once you've both said hello, made opening comments, and asked questions, you may be feeling like a traffic light, that you should go ahead or stop, or that you don't know. The following table can help you focus while reviewing the first encounter with potential friends. The list can also help you sort out what actually happened from what you imagined happened, so that you can better determine whether or not you want to pursue further contact.

You	Them
Do you want to step forward? Do you want to step back? Why?	Are they responding in a way that encourages you or pushes you away?
Are you intrigued or frightened? Why?	Do they seem at ease or uncomfortable? How do you know this?

You	Them
What action did you take to move the encounter forward or to discourage it?	What action did they take to move the encounter forward or to discourage it?

There is a difference between interaction and inner action, and in the midst of a social encounter both occur simultaneously. As you learn to pay attention you will get better at noticing them both, distinguishing between the two and keeping them in balance. It is all right to do a quick reality check to make sure your inner action isn't getting confused with the interaction. Simple questions lead to clear communication.

- "Do you still want to have coffee?"
- "Are you okay?"
- "Do you mind if I join you?"

Here again, old interaction patterns may get in your way when you are trying to pay attention, especially when a previously enmeshed person meets a person who is used to being disengaged. Just keep in mind that your experiences might be miles apart and your new friend is probably just as uncertain as you are about where you stand with each other. Your openness and willingness to check things out and clarify what you think is going on will invite the other person to do the same.

An important aspect of paying attention is learning to listen attentively. Attentive listening is a skill you practice with friends so you can participate in each other's lives without leading each other's lives. When you practice active, attentive listening, you stay *present* with the speaker. You focus on what is being said. You do not form opinions or prepare responses while listening. You just take in what is being said, without making comparisons or judgments. It isn't easy to listen attentively in our society. We are so bombarded with distracting stimuli that it is often difficult to concentrate on one person, one conversation.

> The other day, I was working in the kitchen when my daughter bounced in, bursting to report on her first day at her new summer job. As she talked, I went about my dinner preparations, and at one point briefly left the kitchen to get an onion from the pantry. When I got back, she stormed off, shouting, "You NEVER listen to me!" It caught me up short—the same thing had happened to me the day before when I was relating a problem to a friend who abruptly left the room to get a drink of water in the middle of my sentence. I had felt absolutely discounted.

Volumes have been written on how to listen and how to communicate, how to give verbal and nonverbal "signals," and feedback. Sometimes these techniques, while helpful, feel unnatural and stilted when put into real, everyday use.

Attentive listening is simply a respectful state of paying attention. You can develop your own style, your own way to accomplish this. Often, just realizing you *aren't* practicing attentive listening—as the mother in the foregoing example did—is the most effective way to develop listening skills.

If you notice your mind has wandered, simply bring your attention back to listening. This is not a time to wander even further into negative self-talk, wondering why you can't do this. If you've missed an important sentence, your friend will probably be flattered if you say, "I really don't want to miss that. Would you tell me again?"

Try this exercise with a friend or relative: Set a timer for ten minutes and take turns talking while the other person listens attentively. The listener does not jump in at any time to comment or reply. S/he listens respectfully while the speaker talks without interruption.

Questions: Was it more difficult for you to listen attentively or to talk without interruption? What did you discover from this exercise?

_____

_____

_____

I didn't think I could talk for ten minutes, but I did and it felt wonderful just to have someone pay attention to me. When it was my friend's turn, I paid better attention to her because I knew how important it was.

Creating Dialogue

As part of recovery, Step work teaches us to become comfortable telling our own stories, naming ourselves and our experience without shame. This is monologue. The exercise with the timer is practiced in monologue too. Monologue is good practice, but it is not the same as dialogue. Dialogue is not two monologues pasted together.

Dialogue is the ability to hear and respond to what is being said. Dialogue is an act that lets your comments freely associate from one thought to the next, tracking with each other, moving through topics and picking up on those ideas that are of interest to one or the other of you.

Here are two conversations that illustrate the difference between successful and unsuccessful dialogue.

Greeting Strangers and Making Them Friends

Two coworkers talking at break:

COWORKER A: Did you read that memo that came down from the top brass today?

COWORKER B: Yeah. Do you have a quarter? This Canadian one won't work in the pop machine.

COWORKER A: Here's one. Man, no overtime. I was counting on it too. Guess our vacation will have to be put on hold again.

COWORKER B: I hate these vending machines. I think I'll start bringing stuff from home.

You've probably had "conversations" like this one, where two people talk out loud, to themselves, rather than relate with each other.

Practicing dialogue is like building a house. A foundation is laid and the participants each take turns building upon it:

Two people talking during a break at a genealogy workshop:

A: You seem to know a lot of tricks about tracing family histories.

B: Thanks. It's always been a hobby for me. When my dad died last year, I decided to get serious about it so the family could have something written down. My dad was a great storyteller, but he kept all his history in his head, not on paper.

A: Seems like a good way to keep his stories alive. My mother had a heart attack last month. She's okay now but it got me thinking about all her unlabeled photos in the attic—all those relatives I know nothing about. Was it hard getting started?

B: No, I can give you some information after class. I'm glad you're doing it while your mom is still alive. It would have been fun to do this with my dad.

Notice how each response builds upon the other person's remarks. Mutual exchange occurs; dialogue is created.

Sometimes recovering people are so relieved about their recovery and their new life that they want to bare their souls and share their enlightenment with anyone who will listen. While this enthusiasm is understandable, you may want to proceed slowly and test the friendship a bit before you relate your entire life history at one setting.

If it feels comfortable, it is certainly all right to state that you are recovering. If your potential friend suggests going out for a drink, it may even be necessary to say something like, "Make it coffee and you're on. I don't drink anymore."

> When L. and I first met, there was this mutual interest. I felt like we could become good friends, but I kept putting her off when she'd suggest going out for a drink. I was afraid that if she knew I was an alcoholic, it would make her uncomfortable and all the easiness would be gone. Finally, she just asked me bluntly why I didn't want to go out with her. When I told her I was in recovery and still a little shaky about being in a bar, she laughed and said, "Well, why didn't you say so? I thought you didn't like me!"

In most new friendships, the most important thing is to get off to a good start. This means telling the truth and being yourself— NOW.

Questions: What kinds of experiences or topics are you ready to share? What kinds of things do you want to know about a new friend?

_____

_____

_____

It may be much more comfortable to base your new friendships on the present, on current interests, goals, hopes, and on your insights into recovery. Once you have established trust, you may want to spend an afternoon telling your new friends how you got here. You can choose that time based on comfort levels and the history of each particular friendship.

6

Friends Today, Friends Tomorrow

It's work making new friendships, so keep the friendships that work. You keep friendships by continuing to practice risk, attention, and dialogue. As your friendship grows, you practice these skills at deeper levels. You go to the next step together by practicing *mutual* sharing, *mutual* trust, and *mutual* vulnerability.

As friendship deepens, experience accumulates and you begin to trust the momentum your friendship generates. Friendship builds on experience of itself. The more you know someone, and let them know you, the more experience you accumulate, and that experience sets the tone for your expectation of future experience. In healthy, functioning friendships, the more you resolve problems together, have fun together, share vulnerable stories with each other, and have them respected, the more comfortable you and your friend become. Successful friendships grow through these experiences and exchanges. You begin to know how to count on each other, and what patterns of relating work best between the two of you. You become sensitive to each other.

Learning by Living

Friendship remains vital by maintaining what Christine Leefeldt and Ernest Callenbach, authors of *The Art of Friendship*, call a "learning posture." A learning posture encourages you to keep yourself open to what others say. A learning posture helps you notice how others act and react and think about what parts of their behavior you might use as a helpful model for your own. In support groups, in your circle of friends and family, in your workplace or neighborhood, you can find people who have a real gift for friendship. You can learn from these people and practice doing what they do. Twelve Step programs call this "acting as if."

There's a woman at work, a receptionist, who is the friendliest person I've ever seen. I decided to watch and see how she treats people—try to figure out what it is that makes everyone like her so much. I noticed three things: 1. She stops and looks at people when she is talking with them; she gives them her complete attention. 2. She remembers what they say and asks them about it later— things like, "So, how's the baby?" "Did the meeting go okay?" 3. She is careful of her time; doesn't let people interrupt her constantly, but she spends time alone with those she's really close to. I'm up to number one: I am practicing looking people in the eye.

Question: Whom do you know/observe who has a knack for friendship?

_____

_____

_____

Question: How would you describe what they do to encourage others to be comfortable and open?

_____

_____

_____

We learn how to be social beings by imitation. As babies, we copied the gestures and sounds of those around us. This provided the basics of both verbal and nonverbal communication: smiling, reaching out, learning which postures are playful and which are threatening. We adopted patterns of social language, learned to say please and thank you and to ask how people are. We developed the intonations and shadings of who we are, and decided how we fit into the social fabric. Later, we imitated our teachers, our heroes, and our peers. When we stop and think consciously about imitating, it becomes an opportunity to practice modeling. As Leefeldt and Callenbach note:

> If you want to change your behavior, you can deliberately choose a friend on whom you can model yourself. When you see the friend meet a difficult situation skillfully, you can observe that skill intently and try to distill its essence so you can incorporate it into your repertoire of behaviors; or after you've faced a difficult situation, you may spend a good deal of time reflecting on how the friend might have handled it. This process is not only practice, since we all have much we can learn from each other, but it weaves us into an overall social fabric of relatively constant coping behavior.[1]

Modeling doesn't mean you try to become who you aren't. If you learned to play the piano, you picked up musical skills without "becoming" your teacher. If you learned to play a sport, you didn't "become" your coach. The role of the student of life is to notice options, then try them out, adapt them to fit your personality and preferences, experiment and refine, discard what doesn't fit.

When you want to study how to become more like your real self, it's important that you choose models with whom you sense some affinity. If you are an introvert you should pattern yourself after another introvert, noticing how introverts can extend themselves in relationships. An extrovert might imitate the patterns of an extrovert who has learned how to center inward, noticing how extroverts can set boundaries and maintain quiet time.

If you know the person you are modeling well enough, you might ask if you can interview him or her, or after watching an interaction from which you learned something, simply ask them to explain their action. Modeling often happens spontaneously. You react to a friend's behavior with curiosity, or a friend is curious about something you just did—and you both learn. In this chapter, examples of deliberate modeling, negotiating, and contracting are presented as teaching tools. In real life, you may notice how much of this occurs simply as you become more comfortable in social settings. Modeling does not always require the deliberateness laid out here; however, when you need some deliberate exchanges to correct your course, you have the structure and the information.

Perhaps you are at a neighbor's house having a cup of coffee. The phone rings. You overhear your neighbor negotiating an upcoming visit between himself and the caller, obviously a friend. When he gets off the phone, maybe you say, "Boy, that was clear. What goes on in your mind when you do that? . . . How are you thinking about what you want? . . . How are you taking into account what your friend wants?"

Your neighbor may be a little surprised at these questions, but he will be flattered that you consider his exchange on the phone worth learning from. It is a gift to ask respectful questions because the right question helps the respondent think more clearly and validates actions and communication skills which s/he may be taking for granted.

When you are in a learning posture, the people around you are likely to be in a learning posture too. People right now are modeling their behavior on you. You may know them, or they may be nearly strangers: the newest member of your Twelve Step group, a younger person at work. Your growing strength and confidence in your recovery, and in the new self you are becoming, is attractive. You are not the beginner you were a few months or years ago.

In friendships, especially in the newer friendships you have developed in recovery, you may be aware that you are modeling each other in order to study differences and options. Co-modeling, or peer modeling, enhances friendship.

When I met Barbara, the first thing I noticed was the bright colors she wears—not necessarily fancy clothes, but she has a definite sense of style. As we got to know each other, I told her straight out, "I want you to teach me how to dress, and how to feel confident standing out in a crowd, like you do." She laughed and countered with, "Well, I want you to tell me what to read. You're always making references to books I never heard of."

In co-modeling, you may be modeling difference instead of similarity, like the two friends who trade books and fashion tips. An extrovert might be modeling social confidence for a more introverted friend. An introvert might be modeling social boundaries for an extroverted friend. When we choose friends who are different, who have different skills and ways of relating, we invite one another to learn a new set of skills.

Question: Think about a new friend/good friend. What are you learning by modeling in that relationship?

_____

_____

_____

Question: What are you providing as a model, and how are your friends learning from you?

_____

_____

_____

_____

Modeling makes the process of learning social skills conscious.

> My neighbor has two daughters, ages two and eight. Whatever the big sister does, the little sister copies. She stands like Jenny, gestures like Jenny, walks like Jenny, and copies Jen's phrasing. I know she will develop her own style later, but having a model is essential to her learning. Seeing this so clearly in her makes me less self-conscious about looking for my own models, and providing modeling. It's just part of being a social person.

As these social skills become conscious, new possibilities in friendship are opened.

Making and Breaking Your Own Rules

The early period of friendship is often characterized as a search for compatibility. You have taken risks of introduction, you feel an affinity for each other; now you want to know why and how to sustain it. This can be a risky period because both of you might make compromises to the budding friendship that do not work well in the long run. For example, if your new friend likes fishing or foreign films, you may join in these activities; but unless you develop a genuine interest of your own you'll eventually have to admit this is an area where you are not compatible.

Especially if you are coming from the enmeshed end of the spectrum, there is a tendency to keep proving that you were right in choosing each other, to put the other person's needs, or the "friendship's needs" (whatever that means!), first, before becoming aware of what your needs are and before finding out if you can really be yourself in this friendship. During this sorting process, rules get made, benign rules mostly, but rules you may not even be aware of. If left unchecked, the benign rules can turn into rigid boundaries that may interfere with the spontaneous ebb and flow of friendship.

In the early stages of friendship, you make certain observations and discoveries about your new friends. This is how you learn to know each other. For example, you may discover that

- One friend likes terms of endearment and nicknames; another friend detests them.
- One friend calls you in the morning when you are half awake and can't concentrate. When you call back that night at ten, your friend is already in bed.
- One friend abhors fish; another friend adores chocolate.
- One friend loves to reminisce; another friend gets uneasy talking about the past.

What emerges out of this early period of learning about each other is the formulation of rules of behavior that might resemble one of these:

- Don't call Jonathon Jons. He likes his whole name. It's okay to call Jan "kiddo" and "babe;" she seems to like it.
- Don't phone Bette before 9 A.M. or after 8 P.M.
- Shelly is allergic to shrimp. Never mention the word *chocolate* to Norma while standing in front of her—you'll get run over.
- Bob does *not* like to discuss his first marriage. Don't ask him about the kids.

This list may sound like simple consideration, but when applied rigidly, it can mean you are following rules you have created in your mind that prevent you from being spontaneous or prevent you from discovering the fuller potential of friendships. In the foregoing example, such rules may mean

- You find yourself adapting to a number of unexpressed boundaries, even though you've never checked them out.
- You don't call on friends during a crisis because you are afraid it's the wrong time of day.
- You stop having people over for dinner because you're nervous about serving food someone doesn't like.
- You don't question friends' avoidance of certain topics and don't expect to be questioned about your own areas of avoidance.

When you take a specific example and generalize it, you make it into a rule that begins to hinder how you act and interact, a rule that may be based on assumptions that have not been brought out and communicated.

Often, a friendship challenges you to become conscious of the expectations, fantasies, hopes, and dreams you bring to it. You may be carrying around a job description of friendship, looking for the ideal candidate to fill it. This will not work.

Unmet expectations in friendship turn to disappointments. Unexpressed hopes and dreams turn to resentments. Disappointments and resentments cling to compulsive personalities like Velcro. For recovering people, these patterns are among the hardest to break and the easiest to succumb to. To create healthy friendships, you will need to practice taking responsibility for your expectations, wants, and needs, and for shedding those expectations that get in your way.

Exercise: Write out your fantasy of a good friendship. Go into detail and be specific. Look carefully at what you have written. Are these reasonable expectations?

_____

_____

_____

_____

_____

_____

You need to take responsibility for having reasonable expectations and for dealing with your own disappointments if these expectations aren't met. If you approach friendship without exploring your fantasies, hoping this person will be the bosom buddy who will fix your life, you will be disappointed. Developing guidelines, learning to make conscious, verbal contracts, and handling friendly negotiations are all skills discussed in this chapter.

Healthy relationships have flexible guidelines instead of rigid rules. People in relationships need to give each other permission to change and to challenge those guidelines from time to time. You will have healthier relationships as you and your friends learn what you can expect and offer each other. When you lay a solid groundwork, you become more spontaneous in friendship, not less spontaneous. You act and react without worrying about the expectations and assumptions that might be set in motion. You can have confidence in your shared values, and trust in your communication, so that rules no longer need to be applied rigidly and guidelines are expansive. This integration provides flexible structure within the friendship that allows you to keep reorganizing it as you go. For example, in the friendships cited earlier, you stop trying to bait your hook, or admit you hate reading subtitles. Maybe you go along fishing with a good book and some tanning lotion. Maybe you go to the same multiscreen theater, see two different films, and go out together for dessert afterward. There are many options, once you free up your creativity.

Question: Think of one particular friendship. What *guidelines* are you following in this relationship?

_____

_____

_____

Question: How do you know these are guidelines and not *rules?*

_____

_____

_____

The way to tell that you are following guidelines instead of applying rules is that guidelines are specific and adaptable. You and your friend can discuss them. One way friends adjust the guidelines of friendships is through contracts and negotiations.

Contracts and Negotiations

One pattern that constantly interferes with building friendship is our hesitance to acknowledge and verbalize contracts with each other. When you make contact, you make a contract. Every interaction is contractual, whether it's a smile you exchange with a stranger in the grocery store aisles or the quiet conversation of longtime friends. When you make a contract, it is either fulfilled or unfulfilled. The two strangers are signaling each other: "Hello, I'm not a threat to you." The old friends are signaling each other: "What a comfort to know you this well."

Since contracts exist anyway, making contracts conscious and verbal enables us to articulate what we mean by "Let's be friends." There is much unclear language that occurs in the opening stages of friendship while each person is dealing with ambivalence and vulnerability and while each is hoping the sense of compatibility and mutual interest will last. The desire to step forward and let ourselves be known is coupled with the fear that if we do, we won't be appreciated. We tend to speak vaguely, to overadapt and to acquiesce.

You may remember friendships that started off well and turned out poorly, with accumulated hurt or angry feelings and alienation. You may realize you have a great need to find new people in your life, and fear that you aren't in control of your expectations. Maybe you embarrass yourself by being overeager, or embarrass yourself by being more withdrawn than you intend.

Taking the risk to negotiate a contract can help you balance these personal anxieties and glitches. Contracting and negotiating provides a simple structure that creates a solid basis for friendship as it develops and for circling back and clarifying areas where miscommunication has been present. This is not something only one of you does; *both* of you take this risk. It is not a risk taken only once; it is an active part of your ongoing exchange.

Acquaintance A says to Acquaintance B: "I want us to trust each other." B may say, "Great, me too," or "I *do* trust you." Does A know what B means? Does B know what A wants? No. This exchange sounds like a contract, but it is incomplete. Each person is speaking out of an expectation that hasn't yet been defined. A contract is not helpful until both people have risked negotiation.

Negotiation is a process of verbal contracting. The people involved in negotiation sit down and talk to each other until they arrive at a mutually defined and agreed-upon understanding of their friendship, or of the aspect of their relationship being discussed. These definitions do not need to be identical. They do need to be compatible, conscious, and agreed upon.

Through negotiation, the contracts already existing between ourselves and others are made conscious and talked about until we are *mutually comfortable.*

Negotiating with others is not the same as having a "therapeutic relationship," though we may have learned the skills and vocabulary of negotiation in therapy, in treatment, or through reading self-help material. Negotiation is the cornerstone of new friendships. For a while it may feel stiff and strange to talk so forthrightly to people, but as you see missed communication clear and confidence build, negotiation can be fun. It empowers both people to start getting what they want from the very first interactions. Negotiation is an ongoing practice that will be different with each combination of personalities.

So, Acquaintance A says to Acquaintance B:

A: I want us to trust each other.

B: I want trust too. I know what the word means to me; what does it mean to you?

A: Trust means that you respect what I tell you, and don't tell my stories to others.

B: Okay, confidentiality. You can have that. I want it too. And for me, trust also means you don't make judgments about me without telling me.

A: Like I don't disagree with you?

B: Oh, I expect you'll disagree. I mean you don't decide I'm off the wall and pull back and not tell me why. If I sound off the wall, I want you to tell me. Ask me what's going on. Ask me how I am. Don't just leave.

A: So, no abandonment. You can have that. I want it too. . . .

Now, A and B are beginning to understand each other. They may have been scared to start this conversation, but look how well it's going. They each have more safety because they have clearer definitions. There is already less room for misunderstanding and a greater chance the relationship can work. Every risk builds confidence for the next risk. Later, when A and B need to say something that is not immediately understood, they have confidence in their ability to work it through:

B: Uhmm, I want to talk about the amount of time we spend on the phone. It's not my favorite way to connect, though you seem pretty comfortable.

A: I'd rather see you in person, but when I only have half an hour to catch up, the phone is fine.

B: I hate only hearing a voice. I don't know what you're feeling when I can't see you. I'm always afraid of saying the wrong thing.

A: Well, do you value our half hour chats?

B: Yes. But if we could find a way to do it in person . . .

A: I don't have that kind of time.

B: Neither do I.

A: Hey, I just had a great idea. Let's coordinate grocery shopping. We can talk over the vegetables, have a cup of coffee, and get some of the chores done!

There is no perfect way to negotiate. Success is measured by each person reaching a level of comfort. Negotiation is not over until both people have arrived at a comfortable decision, adjustment, or understanding. One sign of healthy, successful friendships is the presence of ongoing negotiation. In many long-term, happy friend-ships, negotiation is so deeply integrated into the way two people communicate, most of the time they don't notice its occurrence as anything unusual or difficult. Real friends are those who are com-fortable enough, with themselves and with each other, to negotiate.

The five steps in negotiating and contracting are:

Step 1: Say what you really want, what you're looking for, what you have to offer.

C: I want a friend who is also in recovery so I have someone to practice speaking this new language with, and someone who isn't going to be freaked out by what I'm going through. I have my family. I have some understanding longtime friends. I need some-one who's in the same situation I am.

Step 2: Ask the person to respond. Listen to what they say they want, what they're looking for, what they say they have to offer.

D: I want someone new to recovery too, but I get scared we will get into trouble and not see it because we are both fresh to sobriety.
C: What, you think we won't catch each other about to slip?
D: Something like that. I'm afraid of people like me right now. I guess I'm afraid of myself.
C: Me too. What I can bring to you is the promise to help you catch yourself, if you will help me catch myself.
D: It's a deal. I'm not willing to say I don't want to know you because I'm afraid of myself.

Step 3: Express your fears and say what your long-term hopes are, for yourself, your life, your recovery, your friendship.

C: I don't like this being new to something. I've always been the kind of person who if I couldn't get good at something pretty fast, I abandoned it. Like tennis or piano lessons . . . if they didn't come easy, I'd find something else. Now I don't know how fast I'm going to get good at sobriety, but I do know I can't abandon it when the going gets rough. I want to give up my perfectionism, to get more patient with myself and with how I learn things. I want to eradicate all the shame that has built up inside me.

Step 4: Ask them to verbalize what they hope for and invite them to share their fears.

D: I've always wanted to have a buddy, someone I didn't have to pretend with, someone I could kid around with and who would accept me just as I am. But it's so scary. I'm afraid that if I'm honest, if I let you know the "real" me, you'll run away and hide. I want to learn to be "natural" with people, but I'm not even sure what that means.

Step 5: Phrase a working contract between you. Repeat this process when needed, as new issues come up, and when your circumstances change.

C: So, I want to practice being less of a perfectionist and you want to practice being more natural?
D: And we both want to stay sober in the process!
C: Yup, that's got to be our number one priority. It feels a little weird—but good—being this clear about what we want and what we're afraid of. I'm willing to work together on this stuff and see how it goes.
D: I am too, if we can agree that we are free to ask each other dumb questions, or make mistakes . . .
C: Hey, learning to accept my screw-ups is part of my goal! This could be fun.

Contracting is the process of receiving and offering mutual assurance that the relationship is on a track that both of you acknowledge and approve of. Just because your contracts are complementary doesn't guarantee they are wise: You need to run through the definition of friendship and make sure that the

124

mutual goal is mutual growth. For example, if the woman called C. above wanted to assume the role of older sibling who bosses around her little sister and takes responsibility for her recovery, D. might let her do it, at least for a while, but it would not be a contract for a healthy friendship.

You will not be perfect. Period. Your new friends will not be perfect. Period. You will not find a friendship where you never feel misunderstood, let down, disappointed, confused. Period. But you can have some wonderful, imperfect adventures in the company of carefully chosen others.

Exercise: Write out a practice session of contracting and negotiating. Choose the safest, easiest person you can imagine doing this with. (Use extra paper.)

_____

_____

_____

_____

_____

_____

Question: Are you ready to try this in person?

_____

Tracking

One of the attributes of close friendship is that we help each other keep track of our lives on many levels. "Tracking" can be general or specific. Tracking with a friend does not mean running each other's lives. Sometimes tracking means listening to each other without judgment or criticism. Sometimes it means asking, and being asked, evocative questions that help us get back on track. Tracking feels important because it helps us realize that at least one other person has enough information about our goals, dreams, and daily circumstances so that they can share our times of both trouble and triumph. When someone calls and says, "Jay left me," you will understand who Jay is and the significance of this event. And when you call someone and say, "The contract came through," s/he will know how to respond. Tracking also means there is at least one person who helps you remember to walk your own path, who asks how a specific goal is developing, who supports you, nudges you, helps hold you accountable for your stated aspirations.

> When Pat asked me what she could do, I said, "Just listen?" more as a question than a request since I wasn't sure what I needed. But she pursued it. She asked if I wanted her to ask me about recovery issues: How was I doing? Did I feel shaky? and specifically, Were the eating issues under control? . . . This was a new arena for us, and it helped to talk honestly about it and discuss our individual comfort zones.

When it comes to your recovery, you may want to develop tracking guidelines.

Question: How will you let friends help you track your own recovery?

Questions: Which significant events in your life would you like to share? Who might you track with about these things?

_____

_____

_____

Question: How can you help friends track their recoveries or other issues important in their lives?

_____

_____

_____

Facing Conflicts

There is bound to be conflict in any relationship. To be human is to be assertive, to disagree, misunderstand, misinterpret, get confused, or become frustrated. Maintaining friendship requires facing conflict when it arises. However necessary, this can be scary. Prior to recovery, you may have dealt with conflict by fight or flight. You may have sought to overpower a person with whom you were in conflict either by using physical or verbal force, or by resorting to controlling and manipulative behavior, or you may have allowed yourself to be overpowered. You may have fled conflict by escaping with alcohol or drugs, by pretending conflict didn't exist, by using a Band-Aid approach to soothe feelings temporarily, or by assuming the victim position. None of these alternatives resolves conflict. Friends who practice contracts and negotiation as an integrated aspect of their friendship will find these skills extremely valuable in resolving conflicts.

Conflict Resolution

Prior to engaging in conflict resolution strategies *with* your friend, it may be useful to examine the issue on your own by writing about the conflict. Answering the following questions will help you determine what happened (or what continues to happen) and what your part is in the conflict.

• Describe the situation; what did you say and what did your friend say?

_____

_____

_____

• Describe your reactions to what happened; were you angry, disappointed, afraid, etc.? Did you leave, stay, pursue?

_____

_____

_____

• Describe other times you have felt or acted this way; are there any similarities between those instances and what is happening currently?

_____

_____

_____

_____

• How have you responded in the past and what were the consequences of that response?

_____

_____

_____

• In your mind, what would be the ideal outcome to the current situation?

_____

_____

_____

• What response of yours could contribute to that outcome?

_____

_____

_____

• How would you like your friend to respond?

_____

_____

_____

Friendship succeeds when you risk losing it—when you trust your friend enough to destroy an equilibrium by expressing anger or impatience or sadness. I let a friend know I didn't want to hear any more of her pithy quotes, didn't want to concur on any more hip platitudes. I wanted to know <u>why</u> she had been acting as she had. We had started speaking in letters and she wrote me a letter that confronted me in the first paragraph. She let me know she was tired of my assuming I knew her real story—and then she came out with her real story which I had not known. The letter was several pages long. I had a hard time reading each word. Her anger and annoyance would not subside, would not let me off the hook. I had pushed. She pushed back. We got through the confrontation, and now we are closer than we ever could have been if we hadn't risked not "being nice," not being "constantly supportive."

As the women above discovered, conflict is useful. Conflict is an agent for change and growth and is a natural part of being human. Dealing with conflict doesn't mean determining who is right and who is wrong. Dealing with conflict means identifying the core of disagreement so you and your friend can honestly acknowledge it and work toward a better understanding of the issue and of each other.

Question: In the situation you just wrote about, what do you think the core of disagreement really is?

_____

_____

_____

Question: In this situation what can you do and what can't you do to resolve the conflict?

_____

_____

_____

Rejection

Sometimes things don't work out as planned. People you thought you could count on to resolve issues come to an issue they won't resolve, can't resolve, or aren't aware they need to resolve. When this happens, the guidelines of friendship fall apart. You can try negotiating, but your friend may not be able to negotiate in return. These moments of sudden rejection are a relationship's greatest mystery.

Jane and I had been friends for twenty years—since high school. No matter where we moved or where we were in life, we kept in touch, and whenever she was in town we'd get together to catch up. Last Christmas I sent her the usual card and got a letter in return saying that, since we seem to be in "different places in our lives," she saw no point in continuing the friendship. I've tried calling her and writing her and we got together for lunch the last time she was here visiting family. But she was so cold she couldn't offer any explanation, just distance.

In this example, it is probably true that the friend who withdrew is not aware of why she did. Sometimes this will happen to you as well. You will feel an overwhelming need to retreat, distance yourself, redefine the friendship, or escape.

If you are rejected, you can seek an explanation, but you cannot force an explanation *or* a reconciliation. You can only let go, at least for the time being. This estrangement may not be final. In six months you may receive a holiday card and a note that invites a response or your card might be answered. You may bump into your friend downtown and decide to have lunch together. Or you may not hear from your friend again. You cannot predict or control the future—trying to do so will only stir up those obsessive tendencies you've worked so hard to overcome. If you are rejected, let go, grieve, and turn your attention to your other friendships.

If you reject someone, make a commitment to yourself to think about this from time to time until you understand it. Again, be careful not to obsess, choose a time that you will devote to this problem and think about it. Ten minutes a day is a good period of time for problem-solving or pondering friendship. If your friend asks you for an explanation, try to be as honest and clear as you can. If you can't explain the rejection, be honest about that too, saying something like "I don't really understand it myself; I just know that I need some distance right now."

Chapter 3 described various ways to say good-bye to a friend. If someone says good-bye to you, you can also do certain things to let go of the confusion and hurt and move beyond the rejection.

When someone has said good-bye to you, it may feel very abrupt. They may have cut off communication while you were still trying to communicate. You feel unfinished. It's as though the line went dead on the telephone in the middle of a sentence. You're puzzled, not quite understanding, waiting for the line to come alive again. This may not happen. When you say "Hello? Hello?" and no one responds, you have been disconnected. There may be nothing you can do about it. So you need to redirect that energy into friendships that *are* working and into finding a way to say good-bye that allows you to finish, to hang up, to grieve, then to move on.

My friend and I always sat at the coffee table with a big jug of iced tea, lay back on the sectional couch, and talked for

hours. When she abruptly pulled out of my life, I could hardly stand to be in that room. All our long sessions of confidences hung in the air. One day I made a jug of tea, took two notepads, two pens, went to "our" corner, laid out one glass, one pad, and one pen at each place. First I wrote out all my feelings to her—my confusion, hurt, anger. I could tell her in writing how much I still missed her and that I hoped she was okay—even though she'd abandoned our friendship. Then I switched places, wrote out <u>her</u> side to it all. I didn't try to make it the exact truth, just what my heart suspected had happened. I cried in my place, and I cried in her place. The last thing I wrote to her was "I love you. Good-bye." The last thing she "wrote" to me was "I love you too. I'm just too confused to stay and show it." Now I can grieve in little pieces when I need to—and I'm ready to move on and keep my heart open to other people.

Exercise: Make yourself a ritual for letting go. What do you still need to say? To hear? To reclaim from a lost friendship? How are you symbolically going to end this friendship and make way for new ones?

_____

_____

_____

_____

_____

Gentle grief is part of befriending yourself, and this is a good time to remember that you are the most essential friend you have.

Forgiving Friends

Robert Frost said, "To be social is to be forgiving." When you say good-bye to a friend or when a friend says good-bye to you, you learn to forgive yourself or your friend so both of you can continue to grow and heal.

Forgiveness will be discussed in more depth in Chapter 10. For now, think about what part forgiveness plays in conflict resolution and in rejection. Practice compassion.

7

What About Family?

Family. The mere mention of it conjures up a host of contradictory emotions and images: the family as a support system/the family as a place of rebuke; the family as sanctuary/the family as battleground; the family as a source of nurturing and strength/the family as source of abuse and emotional upheaval. For recovering people, most of whom come from what is today almost tritely called a "dysfunctional family system," these opposites can be even more extreme.

There are reasons why alcoholism and other addictions are referred to as "family diseases": The roots of addiction are often buried deep within a family tree, or, even when there is no apparent history of addiction, the dependency of one family member affects and pulls in other family members. When one person in a family suffers, many suffer; and when a family member *recovers*, the whole family has the opportunity to recover also.

The Family and Recovery: Support or Sabotage?

This chapter focuses on recovery and the family: How a supportive family system can aid and strengthen your recovery, how you can protect yourself if your family does not support or understand your recovery process, and how your friends can help you deal with family stress.

Question: Who in your family has supported your recovery?

_____

_____

_____

Question: How have they shown their support?

_____

_____

_____

By definition, a family system is an interconnected unit, for what happens to one individual within the system affects the remaining individuals. Like a wind chime, one member shifts position and bumps into another, who in turn bumps another, and so on, creating a harmonic chime or a discordant clashing.

When you were actively practicing your addiction, your family members adapted by taking on certain survival roles. In her booklet "The Family Trap," Sharon Wegscheider describes the family of a chemically dependent person by saying:

Each family member adapts to the behavior of the chemically dependent person by developing behavior that causes
the least amount of personal stress. Just as the chemically
dependent person is suffering from self-delusion in regard to
the use of the chemical, so are the family members suffering
from self-delusion.[1]

Wegscheider categorizes the survival roles as chief enabler,
family hero, family scapegoat, family lost child, and family mascot.

• The **chief enabler** is often the spouse or parent of the dependent. The role of the chief enabler is to make more and more
decisions to compensate for the dependent's growing inability to
decide, while still attempting to make the dependent appear func-
tional.
• The role of **family hero** is to feel responsible for the family
plan.
• The role of the **scapegoat** is to draw attention away from the
real problem to him or herself.
• The role of the **lost child** is to provide relief from the family
drama by requiring no energy or attention.
• The role of the **mascot** is to provide distraction from the real
problem through humor.[2]

As the addictive cycle progresses, individuals within a family
system rely more heavily on the unique coping mechanisms they
have developed in response to the primary addiction. If left
unchecked, family members can grow so out of touch with reality
that they develop compulsive behaviors of their own. Each member of your family has grown accustomed to the roles s/he has
adopted. *You* may be ready to recover, but they may not be.

Question: What do you think your historic role was in your family, and how did you act it out?

_____

_____

_____

Question: How has your recovery upset the "status quo" of roles in your family?

_____

_____

_____

Addiction consumes families. Sometimes without realizing it, families focus most of their time and energy on another member's dependency. They worry about it, lie about it, rationalize it, obsess about it, try to cure it, and work hard to pretend it isn't there. So it stands to reason that when the weight of addictive behavior is lifted, other family members are confused about who they are and how they should behave now that they don't have to act out the roles they developed in response to addiction. (Their roles may have been unhealthy, but they were familiar!) Now that they don't have to police, protect, cajole, or direct, what should they do? You know how tough it is to give up something you've become so accustomed to, even though it was harmful. Recovery can be hard for your family too.

When I went into treatment and sobered up, I expected my family to be elated. They were at first. Then it got weird.

My mom seems almost angry with me now that she doesn't have to make excuses for me. And one day my kid brother snapped at me, "You've always gotten all the attention around here! Mom and Dad spent so much time bailing you out of trouble they never knew I existed. Now all they do is brag about how great you are—now that you're not a drunk." I don't know what to do about my family's feelings. I don't know how to help them. Until my sponsor confronted me, I was having a long spell of acting like a dry drunk, just to make them comfortable. I didn't have a slip, but I did everything irresponsible that I used to do.

Recovery Is a Family Affair

Recovery is unknown territory for many families. Not knowing what their sibling or son or daughter or spouse or uncle will be like as an abstinent person, the family may unconsciously try to manage your recovery process and control who you are becoming.

Question: What do you think your family's fears are about your recovery?

_____

_____

Question: Can you talk with one another about these fears? How would you bring up a specific issue with another family member?

_____

_____

_____

Your family might be afraid they will be left behind, that you will leave them as you become healthier. In families in which other members are still addicted, there is likely to be resentment, denial, or fear of your sobriety. Members may try to sabotage your recovery by using in your presence, encouraging you to resume old behaviors or by putting down AA and other recovery programs. Still, other family members may want to punish you now that you're sober enough to comprehend their anger. And others may simply be afraid that your sobriety won't last. They don't want to get their hopes up, lest you relapse.

> Sara went through treatment three times. This last time— two years ago—she seems to have taken hold of her sobriety, but I'm never sure. When she calls on the phone, I still listen for that liquor-slur in her voice. The other night in Al-Anon, a man asked me, "How long does your daughter have to be sober before you trust her recovery? Three years? Five years? A lifetime?" It was a very good question, very disturbing too. It made me think about a lot of things.

Early recovery is a vulnerable time for you and your entire family. You all need time to become accustomed to this new way of life. The suggestions offered in Chapter 3 for dealing with old friends may also help you deal with family members. In addition, consider the following:

Be patient. Give your family time to get used to you as a recovering person. You will feel awkward; your family will feel awkward. You will blunder; they will blunder. It is a natural part of the process. It takes time to establish confidence, rebuild trust and move beyond resentment. And by their standards, you may be changing very fast.

Resist the temptation to "shame and blame." Given the family dynamics of addiction, it is very easy to get caught up trying to figure out who or what is responsible for your dependency. Your mother may want to blame it on your father. Your father may want to blame it on your spouse who left you. Your kids may want to blame you and you may blame yourself. This archaeology of the problem is seldom useful. Down the road, you and family members may want to enter therapy to better understand the wounds that need healing, but don't try to sort this all out at the dining room table the first time you go home, six months after treatment.

Be mutually supportive. Each person needs to take some responsibility for the changes they are being asked to make, and to support other family members, even when they don't understand another person's agenda. The past is a learning experience, not a weapon to aim at each other or to use to shoot yourself in the foot.

Expect ambivalence. While those close to you are proud of your recovery, they may exhibit frustration and even anger over the time lost to your addiction. When you think about it, this is understandable; you, no doubt, also grieve that lost time.

Communicate. Letting your family know that *you* know it's hard for them too will give them permission to express themselves. Share your thoughts, feelings, and observations as honestly as you are able *when* you want or need to do so, thereby creating new patterns of family behavior.

Protect each other. Just because they are your family doesn't mean they have the right to mistreat you; *and* just because they're your family doesn't mean you have the right to mistreat them! You are all learning *social control*. Social control is the ability to have strong feelings and still *decide* what behavior to exhibit. Uncontrolled anger, for example, is feeling the rage and acting on it without thinking. Screaming, hitting something, storming out of the room, and refusing to be held accountable for actions while you were angry are all symptoms of lost social control. Socially controlled anger, by contrast, means you can feel in a rage and report the rage, talk about it, tell a friend or family member what goes through your mind while you are angry. Reporting rage might go like this:

- I feel so angry, I could just _____

_____

- I keep remembering the time that _____

_____

- I want to just lash out and _____

_____

_____

- But I know that won't help. It makes me so mad that _____

_____

- After I get the kids out of the house, I beat the bed with a tennis racket until my arms hurt because I _____

_____

_____

You may need to separate from all, or part of, your family as you establish recovery. This separation may last a short or long time as you (all of you) discover what kinds of relationships are possible now that you are recovering.

You may be the one who requests the separation (perhaps using techniques from Chapter 3), or someone in your family might request it. In either case, having the support of friends will provide you with social alternatives, a neutral, listening ear, and the objectivity you and your family need to adjust.

So often we get caught up in the intensity of the moment and the emotion in our families that it is difficult to sort out what's really happening. As you think about how you and your own family are coping with recovery, you may want to write about events to help you understand what happened. You, of course, cannot know for sure what the other person thinks or feels, but imagining their feelings—trying to "get inside their skin" for a while—is one way to gain more insight into the incident.

My Perceptions   _____**'s Perceptions**

Incident: _____   _____

Behavior: _____   _____

Feelings: _____   _____

Reaction: _____   _____

Possible Resolutions: _____

_____

_____

Question: If your reaction was unsatisfactory to you, what could you do differently next time?

_____

_____

_____

You may want to try some of the skills you are learning with friends with your family. Contracts, negotiations, and tracking are appropriate skills for many human interactions, but they may seem very foreign to your family's usual ways of being together. You may find that you can fairly easily introduce these ideas to some family members but that they meet great resistance with other family members, as they did with this recovering woman:

> My dad is still drinking, and the last time he came to visit, he got really disrespectful with my daughter, hounded her the way he used to hound me. I saw my whole childhood passing before my eyes. I sent Jenny to the movies and told my dad he could <u>not</u> do this to another generation, that if he came in my house, and I told him he needed to stop and think, he'd better be willing to stop and think. It's what I expect of myself, my children, my friends. He stormed out and I haven't seen him in a year. I miss him. He's welcome back. The conditions are still the same.

You cannot have a "therapeutic relationship" with your family, even if you think you know how they need to change. It won't work. You cannot fix them, and there is only a limited degree to which you can even help them. The most powerful thing you can do is be yourself—your recovering self. There is an old law of physics: Every action has an equal and opposite reaction. Your ability to be different, to practice recovery around your family, *will* cause reactions, but you can't *make* them react and change. And you can't control how they react. You are only in charge of yourself.

> My sister came to visit me for a week after one more time her husband went on a bender and hit her. I didn't try to make her see the light like I usually do, I just led my life in

front of her. She came to Al-Anon with me . . . listened in. She went to dinner with me and my closest friend and watched how we were together. Finally, she asked me, "Well, what should I do?" and I just said, "Take a first step, whatever you're <u>ready</u> to do." In her last letter she said she has found an Al-Anon group and has the phone number of a lawyer in her wallet, ready for her when she is ready to call. Hooray!

Exercise: Write out or tell a friend your fantasy of what your family "should" be like. Be explicit; add details. Play out the new, improved roles in your mind.

_____

_____

_____

_____

Questions: Is this fantasy realistic? How or how not?

_____

_____

_____

When you know this fantasy, and acknowledge that it *is* fantasy, you are less likely to try to project it onto reality.

Home for the Holidays

A family reunion can cause even the most independent, self-assured, emotionally mature person to revert to childlike behavior. Too often, the skills and experience we've gained with friends melts away the moment we walk across the threshold of our parents' home or get together with our families of origin.

In spite of what we've accomplished in our adult lives and who we've become, our parents and siblings can hook us into acting and reacting just as we did when we were children living in the same household. It makes sense that family members—consciously or unconsciously—know what behavior buttons to push in each other; after all, these buttons are usually installed in our primary families.

> Last Christmas, I went home for the holidays, determined to hold my own, to be accepted on my terms. It only took about ten minutes for me to go off pouting like a little kid. All my sister had to do was say, "Well, you must be doing all right for yourself. From the looks of that spare tire, you certainly aren't starving!" Then my parents started knocking my liberal politics, and before I knew it, we were having a rerun of a million arguments we had when I lived there.

Revisiting home means revisiting memories—happy and hurtful memories. The experience can be both exciting and anxiety-filled. But for recovering people, it can also be dangerous if the anxiety of going home poses a threat of relapse.

There are safeguards you can take to make your visit as smooth and tension-free as possible, and skills from friendship-making that can help you get through family times.

To Go or Not to Go

One immediate tension reliever is the realization that you have a choice about whether or not to attend a family gathering. You are an adult. If you think attending a reunion would jeopardize your recovery, you have the right to refuse. Creating a balance sheet may help you determine if *and* why you do want or don't want to go home for a family event. Divide a sheet of paper into two columns and place your reasons under the appropriate column as you think of them. For example:

Reasons to Attend Reunion	Reasons Not to Attend
Aging parents; won't be many more opportunities.	Stress-filled; always an argument.
I like seeing family members.	I would rather be with friends.
I have the time and travel money.	I've been saving the time and money for my own vacation plans.
I'm feeling strong enough in my recovery.	There will be alcohol and someone always gets loaded.
	I'm worried about the food they always shove on me.

After you've listed the pros and cons of going home, review the list to see what items are correctable. For example, you might want to visit your parents or a favorite relative alone, at a less intense time. You may devise ways to avoid the usual arguments during the visit.

If you decide you do not wish to attend a family gathering at this time, refuse in the way most comfortable to you. You may want to phone or write your parents or siblings and offer either a brief or an elaborate explanation, depending on your individual and family style. Another option would be to suggest an alternative plan for visiting. A letter might read:

Dear Mom and Dad,
   I'm sorry, but I can't make it to Aunt Irene's eightieth birthday party. Since treatment, I've been easing back into

the social scene and her party sounds a little overwhelming right now. I'll give her a call and send my gift ahead of time. I hope to be in town in a couple of months. Maybe the three of us could take her out for lunch and have our own little celebration. Say hi to everyone and tell them I'll see them soon.

If you are not sure how to handle this behavior, you may want to practice a phone conversation with a friend or ask a friend to read your letter to make sure it says what you want it to and isn't unintentionally hurtful.

Question: How would you decline an invitation to a family get-together?

_____

_____

_____

If you do decide to attend the gathering, consider doing some of the following to prepare for your visit:

Reduce the element of surprise. Prior to your visit, take a minute or two to drop family members a line. Mention what you've been doing, whom you've been seeing, how you look. You may even want to enclose a photo if it seems appropriate. If your family does not know you are in recovery, tell them so they won't push alcohol or food or other trigger substances on you. Ask them for specific kinds of respect and support. For example:

Dear Betty,
    Since you and I have the reputation for being the family's great cooks, I just want to tell you I've been in Weight Watchers for the last five months, lost thirty-five

pounds, and have gotten much better at handling my compulsive eating habits. Please don't be offended if I refuse desserts and snacks and bring a salad instead of my usual lasagna as my "dish to share." This change is important to me. Believe me, I remember how incredible your lemon cheesecake is; I just can't have a bite right now. See you soon.

Question: What things do you want your family to know about you prior to your visit?

_____

_____

_____

Question: How will you communicate these things to them?

_____

_____

_____

Question: How could your friends help you prepare for this visit?

_____

_____

_____

Decide where and how long to stay. You know from past experiences what your limitations are when it comes to home visits. If five days is too long, stay three. If three days is too long, visit for one. Be clear about how long you will be visiting so there are no misunderstandings or hurt feelings when it comes time for you to take your leave.

If staying in your parents' or siblings' home causes added stress because the day-to-day or evening-to-evening routines rekindle old tensions, make arrangements to stay somewhere else.

> For years we were automatically expected to stay at my parents' house when we came for holiday visits. After a few hours being there, I'd get so cranky that my wife and daughter got on edge too. Now, we stay at a nice motel with a pool where we can get a break from round-the-clock visiting. My parents always know when to expect us and we make it clear when we'll be leaving each evening. Everyone is more relaxed. Sometimes my folks come over to the motel for a swim, and we get to entertain them a little. It balances things out.

Questions: How long do you want to visit your family? How will you communicate this to them?

_____

_____

_____

Questions: Where will you stay when you visit? If it is not with family, how will you let them know where you will be staying?

_____

_____

_____

You might write or call to tell them:

Dear Mom and Dad,
    Did you know that the hotel near your house lets kids stay free? I thought it would be a treat for the kids if we plan to stay where they can swim off some of their extra energy. I know you love them, but eight-, nine-, and eleven-year-olds are a noisy crew, and I think this will be a good change of pace for all of us. I've got reservations. We'll arrive Wednesday, late afternoon. Would you join us that night at the hotel restaurant for dinner?

Have a support system in place ahead of the visit. No matter how prepared you are, you can't anticipate every incident or tension or feeling you will encounter when you go home for a visit. Putting a friend or partner on notice can provide a safety net and help you relax during the visit because you know you have someone outside the situation you can call.

My husband and I decide ahead of our visits to his parents to take turns getting "alone time" when either of us needs it. If I'm feeling like I'm doing the lion's share of visiting, I signal him and he takes over so I can go for a walk or something.

———————

When I get ready to go home for a visit, my three best friends write the dates on their calendars. They know they might be getting a panicky call from the corner gas station while I'm there.

Question: Whom can you call or ask for support when you need it during the visit?

_____

_____

_____

Question: How have you let your friends know you may be needing support?

_____

_____

_____

Try to keep your expectations in check. Now that you are recovering, you feel different and you may expect that your family will treat you differently _this_ time. Unless your family members are working on recovery issues too, they may fall into the same old patterns of relating to you. Your parents may still treat you like a kid, your sister may still exhibit the old sibling rivalry, and you, yourself, may resort to old behavior.

I went home to show off my sobriety, the way I might go home to show off an engagement ring. See what I got?! Boy, what a shock. I walked into the house, and within a few hours, I was nine years old. I cried myself to sleep in the little twin bed I'd grown up in, muffling the sounds so I wouldn't wake my sister. It was bizarre. I thought I could change everything in one fell swoop: stop drinking and the whole world would be realigned. The good part was it got me into ACOA, got me <u>dealing</u> with the inner child instead of <u>being</u> the inner child.

You can't be perfect. You can't know ahead of time exactly how you and your family are going to react to each other and interact with each other. You can't always prevent yourself from having emotional reactions you don't expect. Neither can others in your family.

I went home for the weekend and my mother spent the whole time crying, "Oh, my poor baby, my poor, poor baby . . ." like I was dying. And my father kept shouting at her, "Oh, for Chrissake, Milly, shut up!" then he'd storm into the den to watch sports shows. Meanwhile, I was trying to make contracts, negotiate a new relationship. I called my sponsor at midnight and talked for over an hour long distance. By the end of the conversation, I'd gotten clear enough to laugh at the ridiculousness of my expectations. I got up the next morning, left them $20 for the phone bill, and came back to my real life.

Question: What do you expect from a visit home?

_____

_____

_____

Questions: Do you think these expectations are realistic? Why or why not?

_____

_____

_____

During the actual visit, the following strategies may help you turn a potential disaster into a probable success:

Act like a grownup. Sometimes we automatically revert to our child roles on visits home.

> Last Hanukkah we visited my parents at their house back East. After a few days my wife took me aside and told me I was driving her crazy, the way I was acting like a spoiled little boy—not helping with dishes, expecting my mom to wait on me, sulking around the house. I hadn't even realized it, it was so easy to slip back into that old boyhood routine.

Make your bed, help with meals, dishes, and other chores and keep to routines that remind you of your life *now*, not then. Express yourself as an intelligent adult during discussions. Listen respectfully when others are speaking. You are an independent being, separate from your family, with ideas and opinions of your own, and the members of your family are independent beings with their own opinions.

Question: In what ways can you conduct yourself more like an adult when you visit your family?

_____

_____

_____

Try to avoid arguments. Strive to find areas of connection, rather than zeroing in on areas of disagreement. In the overall scheme of things, does it really matter if your father didn't vote for your favorite candidate in the last election? If you feel criticized, try to deflect it by saying something like, "Well, it's just my opinion. I'm sure there are a lot of different ways to look at it." Practice forgiveness and overlook past indiscretions on the part of family members, but do not let yourself be treated disrespectfully. Remember, this is a visit, not family therapy.

> I spent the first ten years of my adult life arguing religion with my father every time I saw him. It got to the point where we wouldn't even listen to each other, because we'd be formulating the next point while the other person was talking. It was more like a fencing match than a conversation. Now, finally, I've learned that we'll never convince each other on anything concerning religion, so I just say to my dad, "Let's not get into that right now," and steer the conversation to some neutral topic. Usually my mom is right there saying, "Yes, let's not ruin the visit by arguing about the same old things."

Questions: Are there any topics of conversation that stir up old resentments or induce heated arguments within your family? What are they?

_____

_____

_____

Question: How could you avoid getting hooked into discussing these things?

_____

_____

_____

Present a positive picture of your life. If you don't want your family's advice or interference in your life, try to present yourself in a positive, confident light. Don't dwell on how hard school is, how mean your boss is, how lousy your pay is, how cruel the world is, how hard recovery is, unless you want them to play out their roles as the omnipotent parents or caregivers. In enmeshed families, such comments are permission to lapse into old behavior.

I used to make the mistake of complaining about my kids' behavior or laziness at home. Inevitably my mother, brother, and sister would pounce on me with a litany of child-rearing suggestions and a list of criticisms about how I was parenting. Now I make sure I tell them about the good grades, the extracurricular activities, and other successes of my children.

Question: What positive aspects of your life do you want to share with your family? (Before your visit, you may want to list all these things, to help you remember them clearly.)

_____

_____

_____

Take care of yourself. If you jog, meditate, walk, read, or engage in some other solitary routine each day, do not abandon it during your visit home. Schedule your alone time so it doesn't conflict with planned activities, but schedule it. Staying with a routine can be a real tension reliever.

I try to bike or run four to five times a week, but when I visit my folks I don't exercise at all. My mom cooks these marathon meals, and I end up feeling like a beluga whale while I'm there and for about two weeks afterwards. I was complaining about this at my meeting one night and a guy said, "So why don't you get up in the mornings and run when you go home for visits?" I was embarrassed. It seemed too easy a solution.

Question: What will you do to take care of yourself on your next visit with family?

_____

_____

_____

Take a friend with you. Depending on your family and the situation, you may want to ask a friend to come with you when you visit your family. Generally speaking, people are often on better behavior when a nonfamily member is present, and it might be interesting to get your friend's perspective on your family's interaction.

I asked Mary to spend a few days with me and my parents and she agreed. She noticed things that affirmed the way I feel every visit home—like the way my parents push food on me, even though they know I've been in treatment for an eating disorder. But it was also interesting to watch how well Mary and my mother got along. Mary's mom died a few years ago and my mom kind of took her under her wing. They talk on the phone now, and it relieves some of the tension between mom and me for her to have a sense that she's succeeding with another person my age.

_____

157

I told my folks that Bill was coming into town, and I was accompanying him, so it made sense we stay at a hotel. We did our own things–I showed him my favorite places around Minneapolis—and I spent time with my family too. But I always had someone else waiting for me, so I could break up the visiting into manageable times. Also, when I got back to the room, Bill and I would do a total replay. I learned a lot!

Questions: Is there a friend you would like to bring with you on your next visit home? Who? Why?

_____

_____

_____

Question: How could you arrange this?

_____

_____

_____

One of the joys of recovery is that families often embark on the journey together. The awareness and action of one member who seeks to recover is often "contagious." Other members of your family may decide they want what you have. When this happens, reunions take on a new and significant meaning. They become occasions for celebration rather than reasons for dread.

I used to hate family get-togethers. I'd start worrying weeks ahead of time who would show up drunk, who would start a fight. Then my brother went into treatment, then my cousin. My mother and others started going to Al-Anon. I got curious about Twelve Step programs and started going to Overeaters Anonymous. Reunions are wonderful now. We don't miss the booze and there's this new honesty. We can even tease each other when we slip into old behavior—like the time my sister looked at me in amazement after I coordinated all the games, made sure all the kids were fed, and was about to organize the cleanup crew and said, "And this is <u>after</u> two years of meetings?"

Creating Family

Infrequently some recovering people find it necessary to sever family ties in order to preserve and protect their recovery. Some families are so destructive and dysfunctional, so embroiled in their consumptive, unhealthy behavior, that they cannot support or even acknowledge one member's recovery.

If this is your case, seek to create a healthy surrogate family that can love and accept you as you are and as you grow. In these times of greater mobility, many people have moved away from their families of origin and are unable to go home during the holidays. Celebrating special occasions with friends is a way to establish new traditions and create a loving community.

When you create a new family, you get to use all the skills you learned in friendship. You contract for healthy relationships that blend what you know about making new friends and what you want from your familial traditional values. Keep in mind that you are no longer a child. You are contracting for grown-up and growing relationships. No one is likely to volunteer to be your surrogate mommy or daddy, and it would be inappropriate if they did. However, you could ask an older friend to let you experiment being both autonomous and a generation younger.

8

Strategies for
Social Situations

Unless you cloister yourself for the rest of your days, you will eventually be invited into situations reminiscent of prerecovery, where the awareness, attitude, and behavior of others toward recovery are not easy to discern. A coworker might ask you to bet in the office football pool. Someone might light up a joint at a friend's house party. You might walk into the church bathroom and see a parishioner snorting a line of cocaine. Your mother may serve your favorite sugar-filled dessert. Your boss might give you a bottle of expensive wine as a holiday bonus. As these situations arise, you have the opportunity to see the "old world" in new ways and to choose different options for yourself in the many social settings in which you find yourself, and in how you respond to events and invitations.

You cannot guess when such a situation will arise or when a temptation will present itself. You can only be sure that it is bound to happen, and you can prepare yourself for when it does.

Letting the World Change

Because you have identified your addiction as the central thing about you which *you* want to change, it is sometimes easy to think that no one else—unless s/he is in recovery too—is making changes. It is easy to assume a we/they or us/them mentality.

Many people are actively changing their lives. They are doing things that you would call steps to recovery, though they may speak of their personal change using a different vocabulary. As you cope in a society that is increasingly aware of addiction, you are likely to find increasing tolerance and understanding about addiction and dependency, whether or not other people identify themselves as recovering.

Take a look around you. Pick up a newspaper. Turn on the television or radio news. Lots of people are making changes; they are concerned about what they do, how they behave, what they put into their bodies, and how they take care of themselves. There are people who choose not to eat sugar, fried foods, or dairy products; people who choose not to smoke or drink. Each year since 1980, Americans have drunk less beer, less wine, and less hard liquor. We are becoming more health and fitness conscious, more aware of the dangers of drugs and alcohol.

I began to feel more "normal" when I began to listen to people around me. I discovered I wasn't the only one saying, "No, thank you" to cocktails and asking for mineral water instead. Turning down drinks doesn't automatically label you anymore, as though anybody who <u>could</u> drink does, and only alcoholics choose to abstain.

Notice what's happening in the world today. You are asked your smoking preference in restaurants and hotels. You are offered choices of vegetarian and nonvegetarian cuisine at conferences. You attend events where no alcohol is served at all. All these changes were not arranged only because *you* went into recovery. Many people, in and out of recovery, are changing their habits.

Being aware that others are making choices, requesting alternatives, declining certain foods or drinks, can make it easier for you to do so too. Watching how others handle requests or refusals can be helpful when it is your turn to ask or refuse.

Questions: Do you know someone on a special diet because of a food allergy or physical disorder? How does s/he communicate dietary needs?

_____

_____

_____

Questions: Do you know someone who doesn't drink? How does s/he order alternative beverages?

_____

_____

_____

In early recovery, when you are deeply involved with the issue of abstinence, you may assume that the choice to abstain is as emotional and significant for others as it is for you. This is not necessarily so. When you look around, you see that social ease is possible.

I have a friend who cannot drink any alcohol because of the medication he takes. I've been watching how easily he refuses drinks, how he doesn't feel the need to explain, and, if he does offer an explanation, how natural it is for him. He's not ashamed. Here I am getting all bent out of shape, worrying about what people will think if I order a soda instead of a beer. No one thinks anything of it when John orders coffee. I don't think anything of it! Why should I believe others care what I order?

Whether or not the speaker realizes it, he is practicing the modeling techniques introduced in Chapter 6. He can gain new social skills by noticing how someone else handles the same situation. He is also noticing that recovery is not something about which he needs to feel shame. Addiction is often called a disease of shame. Every addicted person has a certain amount of shame to work through in recovery. You will be much more socially comfortable if you do *not* project your shame onto social situations and assume that others are ashamed of you. This takes practice. You can practice checking out reality with your support group or friends whenever you become confused.

A sense of shame distorts reality. The inner voice that recites to us what it assumes others are thinking is almost always negative. When you suddenly find yourself in a social situation assuming that you are alone and isolated, assuming that everyone knows you are recovering and is judgmental about it, or that they all wish you'd go home, this is probably distorted reality. Reality checking is the courage to ask the safest person around you to talk about what they see happening, how they see your interactions, or to ask them to offer you reassurance about why you should stay.

I was at a women's retreat weekend, and halfway through, several of the women declared that they had gotten what they came for, that they felt finished with the process, and they packed up and left. Several of us remaining needed reassurance that our group contributions were not the cause of their departure or that we shouldn't take their absence personally. Once we talked this out, the rest of the retreat solidified into an even deeper experience for everyone who stayed.

Question: What are the situations that tend to trigger your shame and cause you to question your reality?

_____

_____

_____

Question: Knowing this vulnerability, what can you do differently to get reassurance the next time this happens?

_____

_____

_____

If you ask for reassurance and the other person's feedback doesn't ring true, at least you have interrupted your own negative thought pattern. The act of questioning restores enough logic and perception so that you can now think about the situation more clearly. There is no rule that says you can't take five minutes alone and go to the back porch, the bathroom, or an overstuffed chair to calm yourself. Once you can think clearly, you can trust yourself.

Why Are You Going?

This primary purpose of social gatherings is to *be sociable*, and the skills, questions, and discussions throughout this book should help you feel more comfortable being sociable. The purpose of a social gathering is *not* to eat, to drink, to gamble, to score. If you attend a gathering where the purpose seems to be something other than socializing: WHAT ARE YOU DOING THERE?

You need to understand why you are going to a party, gathering, celebration, or after-hours work activity and you need to understand what the real purpose of the get-together is.

When you receive an invitation to any social function, ask yourself some of the following questions:

- Do you want to go? Why or why not?

_____

_____

- What is the purpose of the gathering?

_____

_____

- What can you gain from the experience?

_____

_____

- Are you expected to attend? Why?

_____

_____

• Will your presence advance your career or help your personal relationships? How?

_____

_____

• What is your relationship to the host?

_____

_____

• Will your presence (or absence) affect your relationship? How?

_____

_____

• Is there likely to be anything occurring or anyone present that could threaten your recovery? How?

_____

_____

• Is there someone going who could help you out if things get uncomfortable or awkward? Who?

_____

_____

There are many valid reasons for attending a social function. Asking these questions can help you define the purpose of the event *and* understand your reasons for accepting or declining the invitation.

I really want to go to my twenty-fifth high-school reunion. There are so many people I haven't seen in years who will be there. Most of them don't know what a cokehead I became after graduation or that I was in treatment for chemical dependency, so I'm a little freaked out about the whole thing. But Sally said she'd be right by my side the whole night, drinking coffee with me and taking mental notes about all the classmates she's heard me talk about, so we can go through my old yearbook and see how they've changed.

These two people made a contract: to attend the reunion together, to drink nonalcoholic beverages, and to be attentive to each other's needs throughout the evening. Later they plan to complete the sharing by processing what occurred. They have negotiated a creative and satisfying way to support each other.

There are also valid reasons for declining a social invitation. If you answer the list of questions and warning bells go off, you may need to find a way to decline the invitation gracefully.

My boss is known for putting on some pretty wild office parties. Spouses are never invited and it is generally accepted that the boss and quite a few employees will get loaded. I will not go to this year's party. I feel strong in my sobriety, so it's not really the booze that's keeping me away. I just can't think of a good reason to go. It's not much fun standing around watching the people you work with get drunk and make fools of themselves. A lot of us aren't going, so I won't be singled out.

If you find yourself in a similar situation, you can say, "I'm sorry, I can't make it to the party," without explaining why. You don't need to lie or create a long excuse. The word *no* is enough. If more and more people decline, the boss may get the hint that these parties are no longer popular. You and other concerned coworkers could offer an alternative, perhaps as an agenda or discussion item at a staff meeting.

> **Mr. Peters, several of us were wondering if this year we could have a potluck luncheon during the week instead of an evening office party on a weekend when a lot of us have family commitments. We would be glad to organize it.**

Daytime parties usually eliminate some of the problems associated with after-hours parties: too much alcohol, late hours, and high-calorie snacks. At a potluck luncheon, you can bring food and beverage items you are able to enjoy, the things that fit into your particular program of recovery.

Question: Are you asked to attend work, family, or friend-related gatherings where behavior usually gets out-of-hand and makes you uncomfortable?

_____

_____

_____

Questions: Do you think others have felt uncomfortable also? Have you talked about your discomfort? What did the others say about their discomfort?

_____

_____

_____

Questions: Are there alternative ways to organize and carry out these events? What are your options and who could help you organize them?

_____

_____

_____

These options don't just apply to work. Creative, new ways to celebrate with friends and family are just waiting for you to think of them.

Your Social World at Work

In any job, there will be some out-of-office, work-related activities you will be expected to attend: luncheon meetings, office parties, office picnics or softball games, holiday parties, receptions, and conferences. You may be required to travel on your job, to meet with and entertain clients, to stay in hotels on an expense account. By establishing new rules and setting new boundaries, you can fulfill these work/social obligations and keep your recovery intact.

In *The Joy of Being Sober*, author and recovering alcoholic Jack Mumey offers many helpful ideas on how alcoholics can stay sober and still enjoy restaurants, cocktail parties, and traveling. His tips for alcoholics can easily be transferred to people recovering from other addictions as well. With Mumey's sage advice to alcoholics as a base, the following discussion has been expanded to incorporate suggestions that can apply to a more general recovering audience.

Addiction-free Lunches

Recovering alcoholics can enjoy martini-less lunches, says Mumey, if they, among other things, dine in new places with new people who don't drink much or at all, and if they order tasty, satisfying food and set limits on the time spent at lunch. He also suggests establishing a regular time and place for lunch so that there is something to look forward to during the day. Arranging for transportation helps maintain the self-imposed time constraints.[1]

If recovering from an eating disorder, you can still enjoy healthy, nutritious, and balanced lunches at a variety of restaurants. By knowing the menu and deciding what to order before walking in, you can avoid the temptation of ordering a former binge food. Many places near work settings develop a reputation for noontime specials: a good salad bar, soup and a half sandwich. Dining with interesting, supportive friends or coworkers can make lunch pleasant instead of an ordeal to be endured.

If you redefine your workday breaks, you can turn them into positive opportunities to converse and connect with interesting companions instead of opportunities to indulge. You may want to consider doing something altogether different at lunchtime: take a walk with a friend, go to the library and check out a few books you've been wanting to read, write a letter to your grandmother, take a noon-hour class with a coworker.

There used to be this midday ritual at our company, where the sales staff would meet at a nearby beer joint for lunch and drinks. More than a couple of us got to the point where we'd skip the food and just slam down the drinks. Since treatment, I've started going over to a health club and swimming over the lunch hour, then grabbing a salad afterward. Now a few other salespeople join me. The health club manager has even offered to give us a company discount.

Question: How do you spend your lunch break during the workweek?

_____

_____

Question: With whom do you usually spend your break?

_____

_____

Question: Are there more enjoyable or satisfactory ways to spend this time? What are they?

_____

_____

Question: With whom would you enjoy sharing new activities?

_____

_____

Question: What can you do to make this happen?

_____

_____

Social Hours, Cocktail Parties, and Work Receptions

Cocktail parties or similar receptions can make recovering people feel especially vulnerable. Free-flowing alcohol, rich food, smoke-filled rooms, can test even the most stalwart among us. If you prepare for these events ahead of time, they can be enjoyable.

• **Limit Your Time.** Mumey suggests staying no longer than forty-five minutes at a cocktail party because "just about everything that's going to happen at a party is going to happen in the first forty-five minutes."[2] Forty-five minutes gives you enough time to put in an appearance, greet the host, and exchange pleasantries with other guests. If you are attending with someone else, negotiate this time limit in advance so there will be no misunderstandings or hard feelings when it comes time to make your departure. If there is a social hour before a dinner, split the difference with your dinner partner, arriving thirty minutes ahead of time.

• **Make Appropriate Choices.** Since more and more employers and hosts now provide nonalcoholic beverages, you should have no problem ordering mineral water, coffee, or a soft drink. Also, as people become more health conscious, many hosts and caterers now offer fruit, fresh vegetables, and other nutritious appetizers. If you are uncomfortable eating outside your scheduled mealtimes, make sure you've eaten your meal before you arrive and don't stand next to the buffet table.

• **A Few Words About "De-alcoholized" Beverages:** If you are a recovering alcoholic, be careful about consuming these products. With the exception of alcohol-free beer, de-alcoholized wine and beer do contain some alcohol. While it would take many more servings of a "nonalcoholic" beverage to equal the contents of a regular glass of beer or wine, the National Council on Alcoholism in 1985 still recommended that people abstaining from alcohol avoid these products. It is usually considered best for recovering alcoholics to stay away from beverages that simulate the act of drinking.

Don't be afraid to talk to your host, bartender, or caterer ahead of time to let them know you require nonalcoholic options. You will not be the only one abstaining from alcohol or avoiding the puff pastries, so do not worry about creating a scene. In many states, bartenders are required to identify designated drivers and provide nonalcoholic options.

• **Concentrate on Your Companion or The Other Guests NOT on the Substance or Behavior from which You are Recovering.** Social functions offer opportunities to practice breaking old habits and to reinforce healthy, new ways of behaving. When you change your focus from your addiction ("Oh, God, NOT carrot cake!") to the positive things happening around you ("Who's going to Greece?"), you will have a more interesting experience and be more interesting to others.

• **Acknowledge Your Appreciation.** After the event, you may want to make a phone call or send a brief note to express appreciation for being included and for any accommodations the host may have made. As Mumey notes, acknowledgment reassures people who may be somewhat reluctant to include recovering people on their guest lists.[3] A follow-up note or call sends the message that recovering people *can* handle these challenges and enjoy themselves in the process.

• **Be Prepared for Hostility.** Jack Mumey cautions recovering alcoholics to watch out for quarrelsome people at social gatherings.[4] As recovering alcoholics are well aware, the more alcohol the guests consume, the more confrontational they can become. When you attend an event where some people are drinking, expect acceptance and be prepared to handle yourself well in case hostility arises. If someone is rude, simply excuse yourself and walk away. Do not try to explain their behavior to them or get into a discussion.

Planning Social Functions at Work

If you are in a position to organize a work-related function, use it as an opportunity to increase overall awareness, not by talking about your philosophy but by modeling it.

• Host an alcohol-free event or provide nonalcoholic alternatives in addition to alcohol.

- Serve nutritious food, offer choices for vegetarians or those who have other dietary requirements.
- Eliminate a long social hour.
- Provide areas for smokers and nonsmokers.

The more often guests are given choices, the sooner they will realize that there are many alternatives to the traditional cocktail party. You don't need to evangelize for your new way of life, you can illustrate it by how you prepare an event, the inclusivity and range of options you provide, the comfort you exhibit, and the social ease you help others enjoy.

I had to organize a reception at a recent conference my company was hosting. I decided not to provide alcohol and to have our local health-food restaurant cater it. They had a gorgeous buffet and had the description of all the dishes set out next to the food. Everyone raved about it. The only complaint we got was that we ran out of artichoke pizza!

Travel Tips

If you are required to travel on your job, simple planning can make the trip recovery-friendly.

- As often as possible, choose a hotel with an exercise room or pool so that your spare time will be filled with healthy activities instead of drinking in the lounge.
- If you travel by plane, you can order special meals when you book your reservation.
- Transfer the skills of recovery maintenance you already practice at home to out-of-town events. Keep to your regular schedule, diet, exercise, and work routines as much as possible.
- If you feel vulnerable to cheating, ask that an in-room bar or snack refrigerator be emptied, or return the key to the front desk.

- If you are traveling with colleagues, team up with someone who enjoys similar activities: see a movie, work out in the exercise room, or explore the city together.
- Find a support group and go to a meeting. Every major city has AA groups, and chances are, you can also find other Twelve Step or recovery groups in the town you are visiting. A quick check in the telephone book or a call to information or the front desk will put you in touch with a supportive community even when you are away from home.

Establishing a New Norm and Creating Healthy Rituals

You may find it easier to develop new social guidelines with your friends than with work colleagues or business associates. You and your friends share a history of socializing. You can change old habits together.

When Rick went into treatment, he let all of us know that from now on, when we went out to dinner or got together, he would not pay for any alcohol when it came time to figure out the bill. Everyone agreed, and in ten years it hasn't been a problem. Now Nan is in Overeaters Anonymous, so we all decided that she shouldn't have to pay for any of our desserts.

Question: List two guidelines you would like to establish with your friends that will help keep your recovery intact. How will you communicate these guidelines?

_____

_____

_____

My cousin has been sober now for fifteen years. I'm so proud of him. I haven't smoked in almost that long. We have the agreement that when we're at each other's houses, he won't smoke around me and I won't drink around him.

Question: Name one thing a friend could do that would make abstinence easier for you. What could you do in return?

_____

_____

_____

Question: How can you achieve this mutual exchange?

_____

_____

_____

Friends get married, their children graduate, you celebrate holidays, birthdays, anniversaries, and other special events with them. These are joyous occasions. You don't have to miss out on them and they needn't be uncomfortable if you use the skills you're developing and if you contract and negotiate with friends to help you at these celebrations or get-togethers.

When Sue got out of treatment, she dreaded the annual New Year's Eve party our group of friends has. Four families get together with the kids and we stay overnight at someone's house. Sue and I talked about what she needed to make it easier. Drinking has never been the focus of our New Year's celebration, so I asked her if she would prefer we had no alcohol. She said that would be great but she didn't mind if we toasted with champagne at midnight. We always have juice for the kids and anyone else who wants it too, so everyone joins in the ritualistic toast. No one missed having wine or beer during the night at all, but we would have missed Sue if she hadn't come.

Enlisting a trusted friend to be on hand if you need support or assistance during a social outing helps you relax throughout the event. You may not need to call upon your friend at all; it's just a good idea to have a safety net while walking on what may become a very high wire.

I asked Bill, an old friend of mine and my family's, to go to my niece's wedding with me. He's been around my house enough to know how my mom and Aunt Berta are: "Have a second helping. I've cooked all day for you. You <u>have</u> to eat wedding cake; what will the bride think? Why don't you dance with that cute little neighbor tonight?" Anyway, Bill and I had signals worked out where he'd rescue me and we'd go out for a walk if things got too overwhelming. We didn't need to use them, but I felt better knowing I could escape if I needed to. I'm going to his sister's graduation party next month to be his backup.

Questions: Whom can you call upon at a social gathering if you need to leave for a while? How can you return the favor?

_____

_____

_____

Inviting People to Your Home

If you host a party, you're in charge, so you can serve what you choose, plan activities, and establish your own guidelines. This doesn't mean you have to be rigid OR be so worried about pleasing guests that you serve things or do things you normally wouldn't do. Remember the discussion in Chapter 2 of enmeshed and disengaged operational styles? Balance is the key here too.

If there are only five things you can eat or two things you can drink, that is enough variety to offer friends. If people ask if they can bring something, try to be specific. "It would be great if you could bring some soda or cut up a few fresh vegetables for my yogurt dip."

If you send out invitations, you may want to include certain information.

When we have people over we send invitations saying, "This is a nonsmoking, nonalcohol home." We find that being up-front about our preferences eliminates hard feelings, embarrassment, or even arguments. Our friends who smoke know ahead of time that they'll need to step outside for cigarettes, and our friends who drink know that they should not bring us a bottle of wine.

This is a good example of taking charge, but be aware that such forthrightness can frighten some people because they may have their own issues with food or smoking or alcohol or, for that matter, with rules. If a friend seems ill at ease with your requests, use your contract and negotiation skills to help him or her feel more comfortable in your home.

What you do and what you serve is a matter of personal

preference and style. Your style may change over the years. The important thing is that you are comfortable in your choices and that you are willing to deal with other people's discomfort.

Questions: Is there any information you feel friends should have prior to visiting your home? How will you impart such information?

_____

_____

_____

When entertaining friends in your home, you may discover that your sense of timing has changed. You may no longer want to host six-hour open houses. In recovery, you are learning the importance of having a plan when you visit friends; allow your friends that same courtesy. Let people come and go as they want to; give them the same permission you now give yourself and do not take it personally if they leave after an hour or so.

If the evening is to be a long one, make sure there's something to do after dinner. Have games on hand, suggest taking a walk.

Now that I'm off drugs and alcohol, I get edgy just standing around at parties. When my wife and I had our last party we decided to get some games going. People loved it! After we played games, someone started playing the piano and a few people began singing. My friends are still talking about that party and how we have to do it again.

Changing the World

What you learn as you handle social events and situations is that you have impact. Your presence as a recovering person, even if you never mention it, changes the makeup of the group and provides a model for people to follow.

A young man came up to me at work and told me he'd decided to clean up his act and stop chasing every woman in the plant. He said he had noticed for months the respect with which I treated woman coworkers and the friendships we seemed to have. What he didn't know was that I have been in Sexual Addicts Anonymous for five years. I had never told anyone at work. I didn't tell him, and I was stunned that someone I didn't even know would notice my new behavior and use it as a model.

You also learn that you can have what you want in your social experiences. You are much more in charge of how an event feels to you and what you take from social experiences than you previously assumed. The more you practice strategies for social situations, the more you create the kinds of situations that support you as you are now.

9

Celebrating and Honoring Friendship

A ritual is a repeated experience with symbolic meaning. A ritual can be elaborate or simple, a symbolic gesture widely recognized or a private acknowledgment between friends. We take hundreds of rituals for granted: standing for the national anthem, shaking hands, driving on the right side of the road, the comfortable distance between bodies in a business or a social setting, the ways we say hello and good-bye. No matter where in the country or the world you attend a Twelve Step meeting, it is likely to open and end with the same ritual. When people gather in these support groups, say their first names, claim their addiction as part of themselves, and recite the Twelve Steps, it creates a ritualized form of relationship. Even if you are a stranger, you know without having to recite a long personal list what to expect in the way of acceptance and respect from such a group.

Rituals of Friendship

Rituals are signals, coded through certain behaviors, about the nature of a relationship. You'd probably be surprised if a new boss gave you a big hug upon meeting you, and equally surprised if your best friend just shook hands. In each of your significant personal relationships, rituals emerge that provide entry and exit to the times you are together and frame the ways you interact.

> In the past few years, most of my women friends have gotten comfortable calling each other by terms of endearment. I like the freedom of picking up the phone, hearing a familiar voice, and saying "Hi there, sweetie." And when they do this back to me, it touches my heart in ways that often surprise me. I feel precious. The greeting reinforces my hope that I can trust intimacy to extend beyond marriage or parent/child relationships.

> I'm in a business with several guys I went to high school with, and when we really need each other to listen, we call each other by our old hockey team nicknames. And instead of swearing, the company lingo is a loud "Oh, puck!"

Rituals need to hold similar symbolic meaning to both parties or all involved. In other words, the understanding needs to be mutual. Informal rituals like those established between friends may change quickly. Rituals are ways we show respect, affection, appreciation, and comfort. Rituals are present at the most solemn moments of life and death, and rituals are woven into our light-hearted playfulness.

In this chapter, you can explore the rituals that have sprung up spontaneously in your friendships, you can design the rituals that support your friendships, and you can develop ritual as part of the fun in recovering friendships.

One Day at a Time

Worthwhile friendships take time, obviously, and if time is hard to spare, a friendship may fail or fall short of its potential. But you will probably enjoy devoting time, energy, and attention to good friendships because they are mutually beneficial. You feel that you are getting back at least as much as you are contributing. But even though it is rewarding to spend time with good friends, time is likely to remain an issue in everyone's busy lives. When you make the decision to sustain and nurture a friendship, you are making an agreement that each of you may make demands on the other's time and interrupt each other's daily routines. Obviously, this agreement needs to be negotiated early on and renegotiated as necessary. One of the levels of compatibility new friends need to address is the question of time.

- How much time can you offer each other?
- How will your availability affect the growth of friendship?
- What kind of time do each of you feel you need in order to sustain the friendship once established?

The most successful friendships tend to be the most adaptable friendships. What constitutes time commitment or expectation will vary from individual to individual, from friendship to friendship, and will change at different times in your lives. If things become imbalanced—if either of you desires more attention than the other can offer—you may want to reread Chapter 2 on balance and boundaries and Chapter 6 on contracts and negotiations so you and your friend can restructure the relationship to reflect more accurately your current situation.

I've known Dee through two marriages and three children. She's known me through three affairs, a marriage, and widowhood. We have never been able to track our lives like most friends do. The phone doesn't work with the kids in the background, and our living/working schedules are hectic. So, we make four dates a year, spend the whole day together, drive out of the city, talk and talk, catch up, show photos, eat lunch someplace wonderful. It's worked for us, though we miss the more usual kinds of contact. In twenty years, we've never been to a movie together, but boy, do we come through in a crisis!

We all have had relationships in which the lack of time withered our connection. We've all had relationships we took for granted and left untended until the relationship died. We can learn from these experiences and develop ways to make stronger, more balanced, and realistic commitments.

In Twelve Step programs you learn the importance of *today*, how this moment is all that you have. All of us have obligations and responsibilities, things we *need* to do. Connecting with other people is a way we fulfill one of our most basic human needs. *Taking* time and *making* time for friendship means sorting out what's important each day—what you need to accomplish, what you want to accomplish, and then figuring out how you can also tend to your family and friends.

Spending time is a minute-by-minute decision. You make plans and then life intervenes and you adjust your plans. This is how everyone's day really goes. Those who seem to forge ahead may be more inflexible and inaccessible to others than you care to be; those who respond to every beck and call may be more flexible and accommodating than you care to be. You are looking for a consistent sense of values and an adjustable behavior pattern for how you interact with your life's time—your life as it is this moment and as it will change.

Here are some suggestions for one-day-at-a-time time management:

When you get up in the morning, preview the day ahead and make three commitments to what you will accomplish today. **Write these commitments down. Post them, or carry them with you.** Your commitments might resemble these:

A: • I will wash, fold, and put away the clothes.
   • I will mail my résumé to three places that might hire me.
   • I will call Martha and set up a lunch date for next week.

B: • I will finish the Rogers report, which only needs a few statistics to be off my desk.
   • I will exercise at noon and eat a salad later at my desk.
   • I will call my sponsor and spend fifteen minutes checking in.

Obviously, these items are not the only things that are going to happen in the course of a day. Do A and B have children? Spouses? Housemates? Pets? Do they have a telephone that rings in the middle of their tasks? People who show up at the door of their home or office? Of course they do. The purpose of the lists is to remind yourself of your priorities so that they don't get pushed aside. A often starts the wash on Monday but it takes until Wednesday to get it back in the dresser drawers. B has a tendency to follow the crowd at lunch instead of doing something genuinely revitalizing.

When interruptions occur, <u>decide</u> how you want to respond in light of your priorities and what else is already occurring in your daily pattern. By noon, the list might look the same or different, depending on the other demands being made on your time. Adaptations might look like this:

A:
- Send résumés before going to lunch.
- Go to lunch today with Martha, who answered the phone in tears.
- Do laundry this evening, and get the whole family to fold.

B:
- I will finish the Rogers report, which only needs a few statistics to be off my desk.
- I will exercise now and eat a salad later at my desk.
- I have an appointment to call my sponsor at 4:30.

You may need to practice keeping boundaries and focus, or you may need to practice extending yourself and allowing life to interact with your schedule.

Celebrate and reassess. Look back over the day for the moments of richness that came to you as you worked your program and adjusted your plans.

- Do you feel good about your level of adjustment?

_____

- Is there something you wish you'd done differently? What?

_____

_____

- How will what you learned today affect your planning tomorrow?

_____

_____

What we do with our time reflects our values. There are underlying values that remain consistent in most of our lives, but how we exhibit these values changes according to the situation.

I always tell my close friends, "You can call on me, even at three A.M., when you need to." Recently, a new friend did call in a crisis. I was surprised at how good it felt to be trusted, and how easily I could adjust my time and still get done what I needed to.

Taking time for friends means arranging—before a crisis occurs—how you want to make yourself available when a friend needs support, even when it is inconvenient, and also negotiating how you may count on their availability. Your friend's dark day may fall on your bright day and vice versa. Even the closest friends can't always coordinate their crises!

I was in the middle of making dinner and looking forward to a leisurely evening with my family when Mari called, in tears, from a little town forty-five miles away. I asked her if she needed me to come down. "I don't want to interrupt your plans," she said hesitantly, but I could hear the need in her voice. I threw supper in the fridge, left a pizza coupon on the counter with a note, and went down to meet her. Mari has always been there for me and it felt good to be able to return the favor.

Question: Imagine that you are on your way out of the house, eager to attend a concert you've looked forward to for weeks. A friend calls, in crisis, needing to talk. What would you do?

_____

_____

_____

Question: How would you ask a friend for time when you need support or comfort?

_____

_____

_____

There will, of course, be times when friends cannot interrupt what they're doing to tend to each other's needs. When this happens, if you have negotiated crisis response with each other, you can trust that nothing is being done intentionally by one person to ignore the other. Call someone else, encourage your friend to call someone else, and offer to get together later when you are able.

Remembering What Is Significant to Each Other

Each of us has an internal code of small signs, signals, and rituals that indicate how we give and receive love. If you are a person who almost never hugs, hugging someone will have deep and special significance. If you are a person who attaches more importance to words, sending and receiving cards and letters is special. One person's hug is another person's love note. As you make friends, you will need to learn your friend's code for affection and allow them to learn your code.

Of course, this means *you* need to know what your own code for love is. This code is unique to each of us and is often based on what we received from those people in our childhoods who were the most benign and life-sustaining influences, or the code is based on what we most wanted but were unable to receive.

My godmother was the most nurturing and maternal influence in my childhood. I could go to her house and it was safe enough to relax and let her mother me. She was British and one of our rituals was always hot tea with milk. Now, years after her death, I start every day with hot tea and milk. It is a way I nurture myself.

Exercise: Take a moment to think about what others give you and do for you that you interpret as signs of genuine affection.

_____

_____

_____

Question: What are the things you do or want others to do that would make you feel genuinely cared for?

_____

_____

_____

Once you know what your rituals are, you need to *tell* them to the people you would like to participate. Handing them a flower because *you* like flowers, or sending a note because *you* like notes, is not sufficient. The gift will not mean less if you tell them it's important; it will mean more because you know they heard you and care enough to respond to you in your own language of affection. And you choose to do the same for them.

Questions: Have you told your friends what your rituals are and how you'd like them to interact with you?

_____

Questions: Have you asked your best friends what they regard as signs of love and how they would like you to provide these for them? What did they say?

_____

_____

_____

As you discover what is significant in your friends' lives—what rituals, dates, events, or objects they set aside as special—check with them to see how (and if) they want to observe these important moments. Some people love to celebrate their birthdays with parties, for example, while other prefer a quiet celebration or nothing at all.

Respect your friends' wishes and requests and be clear about your own preferences about how to observe special occasions. "No parties" means NO parties. "I'd love to celebrate my sobriety with a steak dinner" means just that.

Some friendship rituals may change over time, so be flexible and ready to alter or let go of former practices that no longer fit your current situation.

Jesse and I had this custom of celebrating our mutual birthday by going to our favorite Mexican restaurant, ordering two pitchers of Margaritas and chimichangas and fried ice cream. Since treatment, I avoid those familiar places that became synonymous with drinking. I asked Jesse if we could start a new birthday tradition and he agreed. Now we drive up north for a weekend, rent a cabin, fish, hike, and talk a lot. It's great—and it sure beats indigestion and a hangover!

Sometimes you may need help remembering what's important to your friends. You can devise your own technique for reminding yourself to place a call, send a note or card, or buy a gift for a friend. You might want to make notations in your address book, on index cards, or in a personal directory designed by you for this purpose. Entries might look like this:

CHRISTOPHER

Birthday: Feb. 3, 1952   Loves flowers, hates mushy cards.

Sobriety: Aug. 5, 1987   Considers sobriety his *real* birthday.

TRISHA

Birthday: Apr. 18, 1965   Loves big birthday celebrations and anything purple or green.

JAY

Birthday: Oct. 23, 1948
Mom died: Dec. 3, 1989   Visit cemetery with Jay

Just because you have to remind yourself about these details doesn't mean you care less than you should or that your caring is "fake" caring. The practice of remembrance is a gift you give a friend and a friend gives you; it is not a prerequisite for friendship or a test of the relationship. Again, balance and boundaries come into play. If you establish excruciatingly rigid standards for yourself and set out to remember every special moment a friend ever had, you set yourself up for failure and make it impossible for a friend to reciprocate equally or meet your lofty standards. Notice comfort levels—yours and your friend's—to determine if your attention is appropriate. Or, if your friend goes overboard in his or her attention to you, communicate your appreciation *and* discomfort and work to bring the boundaries back into balance.

Since I love birthdays, I remember a lot of people's birthdays. I used to send almost everyone I knew a card, sometimes long after they were gone from my life. As long as I had an address, they got a card. Then a friend I knew from using days kept sending me birthday cards and Christmas letters. I felt like she just wouldn't let go. I felt suffocated. That made me rethink my whole card-sending habit. A ritual is important when the relationship is still important. There is also a time to let rituals—and people—go.

Question: What important things in your life would you like to have remembered?

_____

_____

_____

_____

Question: How would you like these things acknowledged?

_____

_____

_____

Question: What important things do you think your friends would like you to remember?

_____

_____

_____

_____

Question: How will you check this out with them?

_____

_____

_____

September 10 is always a hard day for me because I lost my baby then. Jane always remembers to call me to schedule something special: dinner, a movie, a quiet walk. She leaves it up to me whether or not I want to talk about the miscarriage. Even if we don't talk about it, it helps to know someone else remembers and will let me grieve my loss.

Creating Friendship Rituals, Ceremonies, and Traditions

Recovery and friendship offer creative opportunities to establish new customs, develop new ceremonies, and replace traditions that may have been tarnished by an addictive or dysfunctional past.

I can remember only one birthday party—my tenth. I was so excited about having my school friends over to my house for the first time. Things were going pretty well

when my mom came into the room carrying a double-layer, decorated cake that she proceeded to drop upside down on the floor because she was so drunk she couldn't walk straight. I haven't had a birthday party since.

If you were this person's friend, you would have the opportunity to negotiate about birthday celebrations and perhaps help his healing process. When it's your friend's issue, s/he gets to lead the healing; when it's your issue, you get to lead the healing. Rituals, ceremonies, and traditions are ways we show respect. The most basic respect two people can have for each other is to respect each other's boundaries.

Question: What ceremonies would you like to bring into your life? (Be creative, inventive.)

_____

_____

_____

_____

Questions: How would you like to share these, and with whom?

_____

_____

_____

Sharing rituals and ceremonies with friends acknowledges important events and passages in our lives. When a community of friends gathers together to witness a ceremony or participate in some rite of passage, the circle of friends becomes closer, more intimate, as they give support and share joy or sorrow.

> When our daughter left home to go to college, my husband and I felt a need to mark the passage—hers and ours—with our friends. We designed a ceremony for cutting the apron strings. First, we wrapped up an apron, pledged our support for Jessica's independence, and had her cut the ties. Then we gathered in a park with friends to exchange new rings, new vows, and to redefine our commitment.

Questions: Is there a ritual you are ready to design in your life now? What do you wish to acknowledge?

_____

_____

_____

You may want to create rituals with a special friend to celebrate something unique to your friendship.

> Five years ago, I was depressed and suicidal. Drugs had taken over my life and nothing else mattered. My friend Ann did an intervention and got me into treatment. She saved my life the day she did that. Ever since then, we get together on the anniversary of my intervention to celebrate my sobriety and our friendship.

Friends can also help each other grieve a loss, note a significant change or passage, by creating "letting go" ceremonies.

> My uncle Jack was my mentor. When he died, it hit me hard. Jack loved the Mississippi River—he lived at one end of it and I lived at the other. When his wife sent me some of his ashes, I decided that I wanted to release them by the river with friends who would understand my need to do this. Five of us went together, had a little ceremony, lit a candle, read some poems, and they listened as I talked about how important Jack had been to me.

Ceremonies connect, cleanse, and enable friends to celebrate and grieve together.

Questions: What ways can you think of to celebrate your recovery? With whom would you like to celebrate?

_____

_____

_____

Playing with Your Friends

There is a bumper sticker that reads IT'S NEVER TOO LATE TO HAVE A HAPPY CHILDHOOD. Many recovering people grew up in households where they never had a chance to really "be a kid." They may have started abusing drugs and alcohol at such an early age they never had the opportunity to experience normal adolescence. It's never too late to have a happy childhood. It's never too late to learn to play, to enjoy life. Friends can help.

Playfulness is especially sweet in recovery. It proves that life is fun without chemicals or addiction. Playfulness helps us see aspects of ourselves that may get buried in the earnest work of the program, especially in the early stages of recovery. When you begin to laugh, to find your situation, yourself, and others amusing, a new stage of healing has begun.

Playfulness is not forced gaiety; it is based on paying attention to details and enjoying them: the quirky tilt of the head, voice inflection, the nonverbal merriment in someone's eyes. Like rituals, playfulness can be simple or elaborate. You may develop a running joke with a friend that delights you both every time you add to it, or you may end up saving your money for a trip to Disneyland.

Questions: What are some things you missed as a child that you would still like to do? Who can you call to do these things with you?

_____

_____

_____

When I was a teenager, I was never allowed to stay overnight somewhere else or to have friends over to my house. Last summer, seven of my women friends—all in their forties—got together for a slumber party. It was just as I had fantasized: We played records and danced, even played jacks on the kitchen floor, and we stayed up all night talking and laughing. Our kids thought we were silly—and we were! It was fun!

In recovery, you learn it's okay to be silly; it's important to laugh. And when you laugh when you're sober, you *know* it's really funny! Playfulness invites you to take yourself less seriously. When you first enter recovery, recovery seems to be pretty serious business. But recovery is a lifelong endeavor, and playfulness becomes one of your new, or renewed, skills.

Questions: When was the last time you belly-laughed with a friend? How did it feel? What was the joke?

_____

_____

_____

You might want to list all the playful things you could do:

- **Experiment with Art Projects.** Finger paint, color in a coloring book, model with clay, do some woodworking, make some paper dolls.
- **Go to an Amusement Park.** Ride the Ferris wheel, go into the house of mirrors.
- **Go to a Movie.** See a movie you missed as a child or re-see a favorite movie: *Bambi, Dumbo, 101 Dalmatians, Treasure Island.* Take a friend.
- **Learn to Hula Hoop or Play Nintendo with the Kids.**
- **Buy an Outrageous Hat.**

My friend Vivian and I decided to make a friendship collage. We gathered all sorts of magazines and art supplies, then we started cutting and pasting things together that represented our friendship. The afternoon flew by and we were delighted with the collage. We decided to get

together once a year for "collage day" so we can see how each of us—and our friendship—is changing.

I had mentioned to Rob how I always wanted to put together model airplanes as a kid. My mom didn't allow us to mess up her house with glue or paint or little parts, so we were never allowed to get models. Rob came over with this huge kit of a P-51 Mustang. It took us months to assemble. We had such a good time laughing and talking and working on it that we've started another one already.

It's often easier and more fun to explore playful activities with friends. You can buoy each other up and challenge each other to take the risk, and things get a lot sillier when you have someone to perform for and play with.

If you can't find a grown-up friend to play with, make friends with a child. On second thought, make friends with children anyway. As most grandparents have discovered, intergenerational friendships provide an opportunity to share experiences, to teach and to learn and have a generally great time. If you think you might be inhibited rolling in the leaves or swinging by yourself, the companionship of a child suddenly makes you a legitimate playmate.

I have a ten-year-old friend—the son of a friend of mine. Jason constantly challenges me to try new things and explore new ideas. We bowl, we bike, we visit planetariums and museums, we see movies, we talk about our favorite books and biggest fears. I like him a lot and, ironically, Jason is helping me grow up.

Moments are fleeting. Moments of pleasure, moments of pain, all part of life's flow. The rituals, ceremonies, and traditions we establish help us acknowledge our lives, help us say to life: "I see you passing, I see myself passing too. I leave this here—this mark of my tears, my laughter, my connectedness to others—to say I came this way."

10

Being Your Own Best Friend

You are the cake and the friendship is the icing. You need to see yourself as the essential center of your life, the one who provides what you need and asks for what you want in the world. The sweetness of life comes from not having to do this all alone. There is a lot of icing out there, lots of people who are interested in being friends, making friends, learning with you. But even in the midst of the give-and-take of friendship, your primary responsibility is to yourself.

In this last chapter of a book on recovering friendship, it seems appropriate to focus on the one person who is going to be your friend forever: yourself. You have learned many skills for taking care of yourself with others. The cornerstone of those skills is the ability to take care of yourself alone.

Terms of Endearment

Being your own best friend requires that you develop mercy and compassion for yourself. In his workshop entitled "Conscious Living, Conscious Dying," teacher Stephen Levine often says, "If you sat down in a restaurant at a table next to a person speaking to someone else the way you tend to speak to yourself, you'd be so upset you couldn't even eat."[1] We continue to be merciless with ourselves long after we have developed a quality of mercy for others.

What comes out of our mouths and shows up in our behavior indicates how we think about ourselves. If you find yourself screaming at the other drivers on the highway, you are probably also screaming at yourself. If you are being patient with an older person crossing the street, you are probably in a patient mood yourself. Judgment and hypercriticism, or compassion and responsibility, originate within ourselves. To become more aware of how you talk to yourself, turn up the volume on your inner monologue a minute and do the following exercise.

Exercise: Write out a typical paragraph of self-talk. What is the language and what are the attitudes you adopt when you speak to yourself?

_____

_____

_____

_____

Self-talk is often generated when we make a mistake, commit a social faux pas, or get confused about what's going on. Suppose you call a friend; you're in a silly mood and start joking with her on the phone. As soon as she can get a word in edgewise, she says, "Uhhm, my mom's here and we're really in the middle of something. Can I call you back?" What happens in your mind? How do you talk to yourself in response to your friend's comments? This is self-talk. It's usually addressed to you in the second person and spoken aloud in the first person. Your response may be highly negative toward yourself: "You dumbhead, there you go again with the big mouth!" and highly apologetic to your friend: "Oh, geez, Diane, I'm so sorry I interrupted you." If you get into self-shaming, you may have a tendency to avoid calling Diane or you might make inhibiting rules that stifle your humor on the phone.

Once you've written out a typical paragraph of your own self-talk, go through your paragraph and circle any negative thoughts or derogatory names you may have called yourself. For each negative thought or name, create three positive affirmations. For example, if your self-talk contains the phrase "You're so stupid, you never do anything right," you owe yourself three positives. These might include:

- I am intelligent and I know what I want.
- I learn from my experiences.
- I am an honorable person.

Exercise: Create three affirmations of your own. An affirmation is a positive statement phrased in the positive. A statement like "I'm not as stupid as I think" is *not* an affirmation; it is more negative self-talk. "I am a creative person and a quick learner" *is* a positive affirmation.

_____

_____

_____

If you do not treat yourself with love, if you do not believe you deserve love, how are you going to recognize and accept love from your friends? Being your own best friend requires a willingness to love yourself as generously and discerningly as you love others. Love is not limited or competitive. You can give love to your friends, your family, *and* yourself all at the same time.

Changing your inner attitude from the old mind-set of shame and blame to a new mind-set of compassion and acceptance is necessary to friendship. You do not have to be perfect at this. You do not have to change your mind about yourself all at once. You can hang on to bits and pieces of mercilessness until you are sure you have as much right to compassion as anyone else. To be a friend to yourself, you need to believe that you have the basic right to:

- Be yourself.
- Be treated with respect, as a capable, competent, and imperfect adult.
- Refuse requests without feeling guilty or selfish.
- Feel and express your own emotions.
- Ask for affection and help.
- Change your mind, make mistakes, admit when you don't know, don't agree, or don't understand.
- Decide when you are responsible, what you are responsible for, and how you choose to accept responsibility.
- Protect your recovery.
- Grow and learn.

If you have difficulty remembering *or* believing your personal rights, copy the above list, add any more you can think of, and hang the list on your refrigerator or dresser mirror to remind you that you are a worthwhile and deserving person.

Acceptance and Accountability

Healthy self-talk does not mean donning an attitude of self-righteousness or preciousness. Being gentle does not mean lacking critical awareness. As every addict knows, shame is an excuse for not evaluating and holding yourself responsible for your behavior. In the midst of your disease it was easier, even though extremely painful, to continue the addictive behavior and then feel ashamed about it than to hold yourself accountable and stop the addictive behavior. Now, in recovery, you have had much practice in new behavior and much reassurance that there is an alternative to this old thinking pattern. As you practice being your own friend, you practice those alternatives.

In the section in Chapter 6 on contracting and negotiating, you practiced being accountable in relationship to others, and helping others be accountable to you. In order to give up negative self-talk, to give up shame, you have to believe that you will hold yourself accountable for what you think, how you act, and how you stay in recovery.

As a kid, I remember my mother using every shaming technique in the book to get me to practice the piano. I learned these techniques well and turned them on myself to get myself to accomplish everything, even something I wanted. . . . When I got into an ACOA group, at first it seemed that my inner child could do no wrong, but I'd still turn shame on myself and badger myself into taking the next risk. Finally, I realized my kidself didn't know how to get motivated any other way. I set off to find out what responsibility, accountability, and consequences might mean, and this has been the deepest exploration of all.

Accountability is a process of acknowledging that thoughts and actions create consequences in the world, and that every human being is in a confusing growth curve to understand what this means. Joe, who thinks he's a social user, says to Harry, "Come on, you're not going to get hooked trying just one snort!" Joe is accountable for what he says, what he does, how he urges others to behave. Harry is accountable for how he responds to Joe's invitation, for what he says, and for whether or not he chooses to relate to Joe in the future.

Accountability is the only way to release yourself from a cycle of indulgence followed by shame or blame.

Pick a recent event in your life—not major, just an ordinary decision to take a particular action.

Questions: Did you hold yourself accountable? How did your self-talk sound? (Use extra paper if necessary.)

_____

_____

_____

_____

Question: If you practiced self-compassion, how would your self-talk change? (Use extra paper if necessary.)

_____

_____

_____

_____

In the columns below, the cycle of inner reactions is laid out to show the range of possible self-talk and how practices of accountability and compassion can radically change your inner attitude.

Indulgence	Shame	Blame	Account-ability	Compas-sion
I can eat anything I want today because I lost 8 pounds last month.	I feel horrible. I'm so undisciplined. I'm so fat. I hate my body.	Shannon knows better than to bring me candy.	I can choose how to treat myself as I experience success.	In the larger scheme of things, this was not such a horrible mistake. I am learning from it. I am already a different person. What a good lesson.

If you shame and blame yourself, you are likely to expect and project shame and blame. If you are accountable and compassionate, you expect and offer accountability and compassion. Your self-love is the same love you offer others. Your self-love sets the boundaries for what you know how to give and receive.

Tracking Yourself

Tracking your self-talk and monitoring the attitudes you hold about yourself allow you to be aware of what you are doing, what you are feeling and thinking. In Chapter 6, tracking was discussed as a function of friendship—letting at least one person be close enough to you to know what's really going on and trusting that person to be honest enough to help you stay on course. As your own best friend, you need to stay aware of the internal realities of your life and to let *yourself* know what's going on.

Self-tracking is a commitment to self-honesty, learning to ask yourself probing, specific questions that challenge thoughts and behavior. Self-tracking is an extension of accountability and compassion. Instead of simply using self-talk to run opinions and commentary, tracking invites us into inner dialogue with questions, such as:

- Why am I obsessing about using again, when I haven't for several months?
- Why am I so excited and nervous about meeting Mel? Am I getting a little enmeshed? Is it time to do a motivation check?

Obviously these are leading questions. They invite us to respond, to be thoughtful, to be honest, to go even deeper to explore questions *and* answers, and to keep on questioning.

Probably the easiest way to track inner dialogues is to write them down. Use two different colors of ink or two initials to designate your inner voices. Start with a question. Respond. Let the next question arise. Respond. A dialogue might look like this:

X: You seem awfully excited.
O: I am. I think Mel could be a really good friend—someone I've been looking for.
X: *What* exactly are you looking for?
O: Oh, oh. Complex question. I think I've been looking for
- gratification,
- a playmate,

- trouble,
- a peer relationship full of give-and-take.

X: Well, you seem to be the clearest about the last thing—a balanced peer relationship, but what about the other conflicting drives?

O: I think I'll be okay as long as I keep balance my priority. My other motivations aren't necessarily bad, but they can't be primary or else I won't be able to offer Mel the quality of friendship I want.

The purpose of self-tracking is to help you maintain clarity so you get what you want and need from your friends and family because you know what you want and need. You have probably already developed a number of these skills as you've worked through this book. Self-tracking reminds you to continue to apply these skills, to make them part of the healthy habits of recovery.

After four years in recovery, I've finally stopped looking solely to others to figure out what I want or need or even feel. Part of my codependency was the inability to trust my own internal thermometer—or even recognize that I had one! I still need friends to affirm me—to affirm that what I think and feel is on track, but I no longer look to others to define me.

As you take responsibility for tracking your life, it will be helpful if you choose activities such as dialogue writing or the following exercises that make tracking a tangible habit. The more you put down on paper, the more room you create in your mind for a clear response and sense of direction.

I got in the habit of writing unsent letters to people when I was in treatment. Now, I write letters to my life—and Life writes back. Once a week, I sit down and see whether I start "Dear Life," or whether Life starts "Dear Larry . . ."

There are a number of ways you can track yourself. Adapt these suggestions to fit your personality and style:

• **Set Priorities and Goals.** You may want to establish daily priorities and weekly, monthly, or yearly goals. For priorities and goals to be useful tools, they must be realistic. Review the One Day at a Time section of Chapter 9 for realistic goal setting. For longer periods of time, you may want to choose six things a week or month, or three things for the year.

> Exercise: Fill in the following phrases:
> This week I will _____
> This month I will _____
> This year I will _____

At the end of each time frame, ask yourself:

• Have you honored your priorities?
• Are your short-term priorities consistent with your long-term goals? Do they help you attain your goals or sidetrack you?
• What adjustments can you make to bring your priorities and goals into better alignment?

If, for example, your year-long goal is to simplify your lifestyle, and your weekly priorities reflect a task-filled daily agenda (signing up for a personal development class, buying blueprints for a new deck, starting to plan the family reunion, applying for a seat on a local board of directors), you are not being consistent. If you find this happening to you, you need to redefine your goals and change your priorities to help you achieve your original goal and stay on track.

• **Understand Your Personal Agenda.** In self-tracking, you can make sure that your agenda is just that—*your* agenda, not your friend's agenda or your mother's agenda or your children's agenda or your spouse's or partner's agenda. Ask yourself:

- What do *you* need to accomplish today?
- What do *you* want to do for others or with others today?
- How will you go about accomplishing what *you* need and want to get done?
- How will you decline requests *you* do not choose to accept?
- How will you allow room for flexibility?

Agendas, plans, and schedules are not rigid dictates written in stone. An important part of recovery is developing the ability to change and accept changes—to pencil in and erase agenda items if you alter your plans. It is also important to use the agenda as a tracking reference when distractions try to pull you off course.

Tracking makes us aware of the fragility of our commitments. We set out to do something and allow ourselves to be pulled aside. We set out with the best intentions and create a mess we never imagined. We ask for something from others and they let us down because they are just as easily distracted, because their best intentions create messes too. We learn to track our daily actions, watching the teetering balance between acceptance and account-ability. As we observe the ebb and flow of our thoughts and actions, we realize others are living with similar shifts and changes. Compassion grows. We learn to assess our decisions, to redirect and forgive ourselves and others on a minute-by-minute basis.

Forgiveness and Amends

If you are new to, or renewing, the process of forgiveness, the first person you may need to forgive is yourself, because in order to offer forgiveness to others you need to know what this experience is. Forgiveness is an act of reunion that overcomes estrangement. We are all estranged in some ways from others. Sometimes, we are even estranged from ourselves.

Question: Are your "addicted self" and "sober self" estranged or reconnected?

_____

_____

_____

Question: Can you separate the hurtful behavior of a friend from the "selfhood" of that friend?

_____

_____

_____

The experience of forgiveness means that you have let both yourself and others off the hook.

I had a new friend with whom I felt almost magic compatibility. We got close really fast. I asked her to attend a business conference with me, to help me cope socially in a setting where I usually felt really vulnerable. She totally deserted me—went off with some guy she was flirting with, left over the lunch hour and never returned. She called me the next day oblivious to our broken contract. Though we've talked it through to where I forgive her, I invest more limited trust in our friendship now. And I had to forgive myself for getting overinvolved, for not being rational, for misjudging the relationship and getting so hurt.

In Step Eight of AA, recovering people are asked to make a list of all persons they have harmed and to be willing to make amends to them all. Your name belongs at the top of such a list.

Forgiveness is a spiritual acceptance, separate from accountability or approval of your own or someone else's behavior. You can forgive someone and still hold them accountable for their actions, just as you can forgive yourself and still recognize your responsibility to make amends. That is one reason self-forgiveness and the ability to forgive others are connected: You can't sort out other people's accountability piece until you sort out your own accountability.

When I was drunk, I did things I thought I could never forgive myself for. I felt such remorse, I got drunk again and did them again and refused to forgive myself again. Vicious cycle. My counselor kept saying I'd have to forgive myself to maintain my sobriety. I thought, "You don't understand. What I've done is unforgivable." But when I began to make amends, to go into therapy with my children, to pay back debts, to finish destructive relationships, I began to think of myself as an honorable person and I began to realize that I _can_ forgive myself.

I cannot erase or pretend to condone the fact that my stepfather sexually abused me when I was a little girl and beat my mother when he was drunk. A counselor told me that forgiveness didn't mean that I was saying "It's okay what you did to me." For me, forgiveness means accepting what happened, understanding that it wasn't my fault, understanding that my stepfather was a very sick man with a very powerful disease, and then moving on toward healing. Forgiveness does not mean I have to love him, but it is allowing me to let go of the all-consuming hate I had so I can love myself and others.

Sometimes forgiveness is the decision to suspend judgment. In *A Life Worth Waiting For!* Dwight Lee Wolter puts it this way:

In order to forgive you, I must have already decided you are guilty of whatever I am about to forgive you for.

That means I have placed myself in the position of knowing who is guilty and who is not. Then I decide if you are to be punished or forgiven. I have adorned myself with a crown of resentments. I am the standard against which all goodness is measured. I am a self-appointed judge and exe-cutioner. I have relieved God of most of his duties.

I sit and wonder how I can forgive my parents without having judged them guilty. I can't. Guilty of what? Of having been ill? Of having been born into a bad family situation the same way I was?

I cannot forgive my parents if I cannot forgive myself. The executioner who screams, "Off with their heads!" every time I discover yet another way in which my parents couldn't properly nurture me is the same executioner who is out to get me every time I make a mistake. The executioner does not discriminate against me or others. The executioner wants blood. Any blood. The only way for me to be spared is to declare an unconditional amnesty for all prisoners of the disease. Then I and my parents and my friends and all the wounded, defensive people who suffer in silence and fear of retribution can come out and talk about what happened and where to go from here.

I am raising the white flag of enlightened surrender. Getting back, or getting over, or getting even is not the name of the game. The name of the game is LEARNING TO LOVE AND LIVE. Let's get on with it.[2]

The Spiritual Value of Friendship

The more deeply you engage in it, the more recovery becomes an immensely sophisticated and satisfying life process. In the beginning stages, many people think recovery consists of stopping an identified addictive behavior. "I am in recovery," we say proudly, meaning, "I haven't had a drink, a snort, or a binge for x amount of time." However, the longer we live as recovering persons, the more we understand that recovery is a code word for reclaiming our entire lives.

As we live with the process of reclamation, we realize that our own growth, our friendships, and our perceptions of what's happening need finally to be placed in a spiritual context because that is the only context in which we can understand our lives. When we do this, four truisms emerge.

1. It takes a long time, and a decision to look honestly at ourselves, to gain understanding of what's happening and why.
2. We are always midstream, with new information floating by all the time, creating better understanding and reconfirming our insights.
3. The "answers" are only temporary and the best of these take the spiritual dimensions into account.
4. We are ultimately responsible *for* the nature of the journey we make out of our lives, and responsible *to* those who travel with us.

Recovery is a circular process that revolves from the center of self to others and then back again. We recognize the need for external and internal guidance. We reach out to others and to a Higher Power, and with this companionship and the knowledge we gain, we get to know others and ourselves better.

Buddhists speak of making daily acts into meditations, making mindless moments mindful. If you are eating mindfully, it becomes eating meditation; if you are walking with careful focus on the physical act of lifting and placing your feet, it becomes walking meditation. Spiritual work occurs whenever we are mindful of a remark made and received, of a hug exchanged, of a thought or feeling explored, of a suggestion reciprocated. The spiritual context that provides us with insight is a state of awareness available to us always.

In your relationship to yourself, and in friendships based solidly on practices of recovery, this state of mindfulness comes more and more naturally. The spiritual breaks through our blinders to make ordinary moments richer.

All the friendships I have developed in the past five years, since starting Al-Anon and recovering in a number of ways, have a distinct aspect to them that I don't share with old friends or family. In these new relationships, at one time or another, we have touched each other's hearts. There has been a smile exchanged, a long comfortable hug, tears acknowledged. . . . I did these things before, but now I know how to do them with my heart open. And after that, even if we don't talk about it, we trust each other more.

This moment of openheartedness is true integration of action and reflection. It is mindfulness.

Question: In what ways do you acknowledge the spiritual nature of friendship?

_____

_____

_____

Question: How do you and your friends experience an open heart toward each other?

_____

_____

_____

The spiritual dimension reinforces a sense of living midstream. All the anonymous comments throughout these pages are comments on lives and relationships *in process.* Even those relationships that appear finished on the social level may continue to grow and change on a spiritual level. The long process of peacemaking with your past and present has necessitated saying goodbye to some people, hello to others. You learn to ask yourself, over and over, what is the gift? What is the lesson?

As you prepare to take further steps in friendship, the spiritual dimension enables the asking of questions that can guide you forward. Think now of a good friend and answer honestly these questions:

Question: How do you wish to be thought of and remembered in this friend's life?

_____

_____

_____

Question: How do you wish to think of and remember this friend?

_____

_____

_____

Questions: How do you need to interact with your friend? How do you need to conduct yourself in order for these desires to be fulfilled?

_____

_____

_____

Question: What are the spiritual components to the exchanges you make or have made with each other?

_____

_____

_____

Sometimes we can be friends a long time before the spiritual dimensions of a relationship emerge, and sometimes the spiritual dimensions emerge first. A good friendship—a balanced, loving, mutual relationship—is like being shown a piece of God. Friends are capable of showing us how real this Power is and how much our souls desire this spiritual connection. The times when our friends provide just the right aspect of love and support give us concrete examples of what goodness really is and help us develop a model for offering goodness to the next person in need.

In recovery, every friendship is a new one—whether you are saying hello for the first time or you have known the person all your life. Every friendship is new because *you* are new and you are living a new kind of life. This is a marvelous path you have chosen, and you travel in good company. You journey with the best friend you will ever have: yourself. Dare to proceed.

Notes

1. Coming into the World

1. Anne Geller, M.D., *Restore Your Life: A Living Plan for Sober People* (New York: Bantam, 1991), p. 4.

2. Taking the First Step to Friendship

1. Terence Gorski, *Passages Through Recovery* (San Francisco: Harper & Row, 1989), p. 54.
2. Anne Wilson Schaef, *Co-dependence: Misunderstood, Mistreated* (Minneapolis: Winston Press, 1986), p. 45.
3. Craig Nakken, *The Addictive Personality* (Minneapolis: Hazelden, 1988), p. 11.
4. Salvador Minuchin, *Families and Family Systems Therapy* (Cambridge, MA: Harvard University Press, 1974), p. 54
5. Ibid. p. 55.

4. Making New Friends

1. Anne Geller, M.D., *Restore Your Life: A Living Plan for Sober People* (New York: Bantam, 1991), pp. 198–99.
2. Ibid. pp. 198–99.

5. Greeting Strangers and Making Them Friends

1. Leonard Zunin and Natalie Zunin, *Contact: The First Four Minutes* (Los Angeles: Nash Publishing, 1972).

6. Friends Today, Friends Tomorrow

1. Christine Leefeldt and Ernest Callenbach, *The Art of Friendship* (New York: Pantheon Books, 1979), pp. 210–11.

7. What About Family?

1. Sharon Wegscheider, "The Family Trap" (St. Paul, MN: Nurturing Networks, 1976), p. 3.
2. Ibid. pp. 7, 9, 11, 13, 15, 17.

8. Strategies for Social Situations

1. Jack Mumey, *The Joy of Being Sober* (Chicago: Contemporary Books, 1984), pp. 123–29.
2. Ibid. p. 140.
3. Ibid. p. 142.
4. Ibid. p. 143.

10. Being Your Own Best Friend

1. Stephen Levine, cassette transcription from workshop.
2. Dwight Lee Wolter, *A Life Worth Waiting For!* (Minneapolis: CompCare Publishers, 1989), p. 224.

Recommended Readings

Recovery and Codependency

Geller, Anne. *Restore Your Life: A Living Plan for Sober People.* New York: Bantam, 1991.

Gorski, Terence. *Passages Through Recovery.* San Francisco: Harper & Row, 1989.

Mumey, Jack. *The Joy of Being Sober.* Chicago: Contemporary Books, 1984.

Nakken, Craig. *The Addictive Personality.* Minneapolis: Hazelden, 1988.

Orange, Cynthia. "Addicts and Families in Recovery." Minneapolis: Hazelden, 1986.

Schaef, Anne Wilson. *Co-dependence: Misunderstood, Mistreated.* Minneapolis: Winston Press, 1986.

———. *When Society Becomes an Addict.* San Francisco: Harper & Row, 1987.

Friendship

Burns, David. *Intimate Connections*. New York: William Morrow, 1985.

Leefeldt, Christine, and Ernest Callenbach. *The Art of Friendship*. New York: Pantheon Books, 1979.

Minuchin, Salvador. *Families and Family Systems Therapy*. Cambridge, MA: Harvard University Press, 1974.

Pogrebin, Letty Cottin. *Among Friends*. New York: McGraw-Hill, 1987.

Powell, John. *Why am i afraid to tell you who i am?* Niles, IL: Argus Communications, 1969.

Wegscheider, Sharon. "The Family Trap." St. Paul, MN: Nurturing Networks, 1976.

Zunin, Leonard, and Natalie Zunin. *Contact: The First Four Minutes*. Los Angeles: Nash Publishing, 1972.

Next Steps: More Good Things to Think About

Baldwin, Christina. *One to One: Self-Understanding Through Journal Writing*. New York: M. Evans & Co., 1977/1991.

———. *Life's Companion: Journal Writing as a Spiritual Quest*. New York: Bantam, 1990.

Levine, Stephen. *Healing into Life and Death*. New York: Doubleday, 1987.

Miller, Alice. *Banished Knowledge: Facing Childhood Injuries*. New York: Doubleday, 1990.

Orange, Cynthia. "Emotional Maturity." Minneapolis: Hazelden, 1985.

———. "Reclaiming Personal Power." Minneapolis: Hazelden, 1985.

Wolter, Dwight Lee. *A Life Worth Waiting For!* Minneapolis: CompCare Publishers, 1989.